COUNSEL to the CHRIST
Also
MEDITATIONS & EXPERIENCES

Made Public, as a Testimony
to the Right Way to God,
Revealed and Made Known in this
the Day of his Glorious Appearing
to his People. That they may be
Encouraged to Walk therein
to the End thereof.

By William Shewen

Exodus 14:15   Speak unto the children of Israel,
that they go forward.
Matthew 10:22 He that endures to the end, shall be saved.

London, Printed by John Bringhurst,
At the Sign of the Book in Grace-Church-Street
1683
Reprinted in whole, or just the Meditations:
1764, 1769, 1771, 1793, 1799, 1826, 1827, 1838,

Reprinted
Inner Light Books
San Francisco, California
2008

Printing History of the text.

First Printed as:

COUNSEL to the CHRISTIAN-TRAVELLER: also *Meditations and Experiences* made public, as a TESTIMONY to the Right Way of God, Revealed and made known in this Day of his Glorious Appearing in his People That they may be encouraged to walk therein to the end thereof.
By *W. Shewen*.

> Exod. xiv. xv.—*Speak unto the children of Israel, that they go forward.*

> Mat. x. xxii—*He that indureth to the End, shall be saved.*

London, Printed by John Bringhurst, at the sign of the Book in Grace-church-street   8vo. 1683

Reprinted.

> *London: Printed and sold by Luke Hinde, at the Bible, in George-yard, Lombard Street.*
> 8vo. 1764.

Reprinted.—The 3rd edition, revised and corrected. To which is added, "A Treatise concerning Thoughts and Imaginations, good and evil; also a few words concerning the Life of a Christian, and Christian worship."

> *London: Printed and sold by Mary Hinde, at No. 2, in George-yard, Lombard-street.* 8vo. 1769.

Reprinted.—The 4th edition, revised and corrected. To which is added, A treatise concerning Thoughts and Imaginations, &c. By W. Shewen.

> *Dublin: Printed and sold by Isaac Jackson and Son, at the Globe in Meath-street.*
> Large 12mo. 1771.

Reprinted.—(America)

> *Salem: Printed by Thomas C. Cushing; sold by W. Carlton, at the Bible and Heart.*
> 8vo. 1793.

Reprinted.—Without, "The Meditations, &c. the 4th edition.

> *London: Printed and sold by James Phillips & Son, George-yard, Lombard-street.*
> 12mo. 1799.

Reprinted.—The 6th edition.   *Dublin*   1827.

Meditations and Experiences, &c., &c., by William Shewen.

> Taken from the Third Edition, printed 1769.

> *Bradford: Printed by W.H. Blackburn*   24mo.   1826.

The same, called the 5th edition.

> *Manchester: Printed by John Harrison, Market Street.*

For the Manchester and Stockport Tract Depository and Association, &c., &c.

> 24mo.   1838.

Meditations and Experiences, &c., &c., by William Shewen.

> (Taken from the Third Edition, printed 1769.)

> *Mossley: Printed by W. B. Micklethwaite for S. Bradburn, Mealhouse Brow, Stockport.*
> 12mo. *No date.*

> Note.—There is inserted in this edition "A Letter to Benjamin Bangs by W. Rylance," dated, "Breerton, 11 mo. 30th, 1722."

Reprinted as

COUNSEL to the CHRISTIAN-TRAVELLER: also *Mediations and Experiences* by William Shewen

Published by Inner Light Books, San Francisco, California

Copyright © 2008 Inner Light Books

http://www.innerlightbooks.com

email: editor@innerlightbooks.com

ISBN 978-0-9797110-0-8 (hardcover)

ISBN 978-0-9797110-1-5 (softcover)

COUNSEL to the CHRISTIAN-TRAVELLER:
Also
MEDITATIONS & EXPERIENCES

Table of Contents

A Note about the Author
William Shewen

The following excerpt is from the preface to the 1826 edition of William Shewen's *Meditations and Experiences*.

"In pursuing the present valuable little work, it may be interesting to the reader to be put in possession of the following brief notice of the author, by George Whiting, who was personally acquainted with him. Advertising to the events of 1695, he says:

'This year died William Shewen, of London. He was a very serviceable man on Truth's account, several ways, and an elder in the church, of a sound judgment and understanding in the Truth, and had very clear openings in relation to the work of it; and, also, of Satan's wiles to hurt and hinder the progress in it, having had long experience of both, and therefore could advise and direct the Christian Traveler, how to keep in the one, and be preserved out of the Snares of the other; and wrote in peace with the Lord, and in unity with his people, the 28th of 5th month, 1695, about 64 years of age.' From page 505 of George Whiting's Memoirs, 2nd edition."

William Shewen was born around 1631. He lived in London on the south bank of the Thames and was a member of Southwark Monthly Meeting. In 1656 his house in Bermondsey Street (at the sign of the two brewers) was one of the first meeting places of Friends south of the river, according to Norman Penney in his book, *First Publishers of Truth*. The index to The Journal of Friends Historical Society describes Shewen as a pin maker of Bermondsey, Surrey and Enfield, Middlesex. In 1679 Shewen married Ann Raper with whom he had three children.

William Shewen was a member of Meeting for Sufferings in the 1670s and 80s and was appointed to deliver papers to the judges of assize, to attend Parliament in session and is signatory to a number of public documents and letters. He was one of those appointed to negotiate through merchants with the kidnappers of Quakers, held captive in Algiers, and to appeal for funds from Friends to ransom them. He acted as umpire in a dispute between Ellis Hookes (the first Recording Clerk) and the Quaker printer Andrew Soul in 1679/80 that

A Note about the Author

resulted in official printing being taken away from Soul. There seems also to be evidence that he wrote letters for Hookes on behalf of the Meeting. In fact Shewen and Hookes (who came from the same area of London) seem to have been close - he was one of those given bequests in Hookes' will in 1681.

Shewen was an early-convinced Friend and a prominent member of the Religious Society of Friends in London in the mid to late seventeenth century; he was also the author of a number of tracts and books. In 1674 Shewen began quarreling in public with Jeremiah Ives, a Baptist. The quarrel escalated into an exchange of pamphlets that began Shewen's career as a writer. In Smith's *Descriptive Catalogue of Friends' Books*, there are ten entries for William Shewen, some of the works being reprinted up to the middle of the nineteenth century,

The Horslydown Meeting (also called the Southwark Meeting) of which Shewen was an active member from the year 1654 was a focus of persecution by the civil authorities. As described in Braithwaite's *The Second Period of Quakerism*, in 1670 the Meeting House was torn down by order of the Lord Mayor. The Horslydown Friends continued holding Meeting on the ruins and the authorities harassed and abused them over a four-week period. It was reported that "twenty, thirty, fifty, and twenty persons were wounded, sorely bruised and blood spilt" is the attempt to discourage the Friends from meeting. In February 1671 the persecution stopped after it was "sufficiently proved, (that) no human power nor any penalties could deter them." In 1683, as recorded in Besse's *A Collection of the Sufferings of the People called Quakers*, Shewen along with other members of the Horslydown Meeting were arrested when after being barred from holding Meeting for Worship in their Meeting House they held the Meeting in the street.

In both his work with the Meeting for Sufferings and his personal experience of persecution Shewen came to champion the freedom of conscience and religious practice. William Shewen died on 28 Fifth Month 1695 in Enfield, Middlesex, England.

TO THE
Christian Reader.

I do not mean you that has only the name CHRISTIAN, because you have been born in a nation called so, or because your parents were so, and that you have walked in their traditions, and made profession of that which is reputed the Christian religion: neither do I mean you, that are the son, daughter, servant, or hand-maid of a Christian indeed, who has been trained up, educated, and instructed in the principles of the Christian religion, not only by precept, but by example; and has in honor and respect to your parents and master, yielded obedience so far, as to walk in some measure in the form thereof, out of the superfluity of naughtiness that is in the world, which is commendable in its place, time, and season: yet you are not the Christian I here intend. But you are the man or woman, who has known something of the work and power of God in or upon your heart, mind, and conscience, and are in some measure quickened, and made alive thereby; and has been made sensible of your harsh bondage and captivity; and has cries and breathings begotten in you for deliverance, under the sense of the sad estate and condition, without a Savior: you to whom sin has been a grievous burden with which you have been weary and heavy laden: You, to whom sin is made exceeding sinful; so that you hate it even as God hates it, that is, because it is sin; and are in love with righteousness, purity, and holiness, having felt the drawings of the Father to the Son, your Savior; and you are now in Him, pressing hard to be wholly freed from the one, and to become a servant, child, and friend of the other.

You are the Christian reader my heart yearns towards, my care is for, and my advice is to, that you may persevere to the end, and escape all the dangers in the way; that you may be acquainted with the wiles of the enemy, and with his mysterious working against you, even after the strong man is bound, his goods spoiled, and your house swept and garnished; after you have clean escaped the pollution of the world, and the errors therein, and have had much experience of the power and presence of the Lord; even after he has brought you in his vineyard, into his garden, and made you a cultivator and care taker of it, and a laborer in it: if you will receive and keep the penny, the reward, you must be diligent and watchful therein. And remember, the serpent came into Paradise to deceive; and that Satan came before God, to accuse and stir him up against the righteous; and that the great Red Dragon got into Heaven; and not only so, but made war there, and stood before the woman which was ready to be delivered, to devour her child so soon as it was born. And when he was over-come in Heaven, and cast into the earth and sea, and among the inhabitants thereof, he ceases not to be wrath with the woman, and to make war with the remnant of her seed, which keep the Commandments of God, and have the Testimony of Jesus. Read Revelations 12. This has been his work of old, and is the same at this day.

Now, seeing Paradise, the presence of God and Heaven, are not exempted from the approaches of the Serpent, Satan, and Dragon; what great need is there for you to be always armed against him, and to keep a watchful eye over him (especially when he appears as your friend, as he did in Paradise, when he said, you shall not die, you shall be as gods; as if he had said, I am so much your friend, that I am come to persuade you to do something to better your estates, and to bring you into a greater glory: I propose nothing, only that, if you obey me, shall turn to your good. Thus he deceived them then; and has done since, and may do so again, if you abide not in the Light which discovers him, and all his wiles and devices, forming and transformations.) But as your eye is single, you will always see and know him to be as he is, and not as he appears to be: so shall you never be deceived, nor betrayed by him. But many assaults, trials, and temptations, you must expect from him: amidst of all, keep your eye upon God your Savior, who has given you faith in him; which faith is indeed very precious, and very powerful, able to overcome, and give you victory over all your enemies. If you care for it, and grow in it, it will certainly be as an anchor to you, when storms attend; as a shield and breastplate to you, when enemies assault. And remember the counsel of Paul, Silvanus and Timotheus to the Thessalonians, let us who are of the day be sober, putting on the breast-plate of faith and love, and for a helmet the hope of Salvation; for God has not appointed us to wrath, but to obtain Salvation by our Lord Jesus Christ. This was the blessed end of the call and appointment of God in all ages; specifically that all that hear and obey it might obtain Salvation, the end of faith and hope; and it is the same to a remnant in this age: happy are you that enjoy it, and abide with him that has called you to it, and wrought it in you, and for you, which is God blessed and praised throughout all generations.

Now Christian reader, what I have here committed to the press, is from a deep and weighty consideration, observation, experience and knowledge of the glorious appearance of God in this our day, in the hearts, minds and consciences of thousands, who have been made as clay in the hand of the potter, ready to be made and formed according to his will, even vessels of honor, and many have been made so, and do so remain; but some have been marred, even upon the wheel, some have miscarried in the midst of the way, some have sat down in the way, some have fallen out (even with their brethren) by the way, some have turned out of the way, and brought an evil report upon the way, and have laid stumbling blocks in the way; and occasioned the way of Truth to be spoken evil of, whose damnation slumbers not: my hearty desire is, that neither you, nor I may ever be of this number; so what I say to you, I say to my own soul, go forward to perfection, let not the enemy of your soul deceive you of your exceeding great reward, which is laid up in store for all that love the appearance of God in Christ Jesus, and that join therewith, and work therein, until all the works of sin, self and Satan are wrought out and destroyed; and you are fully delivered from the bondage of corruption, into the glorious liberty of the Children of God, which you have longed for and breathed after and are now called to the possession and enjoyment of; and not only so, but to the abiding and standing fast therein, so that you shall never be entangled with the yoke of bondage again, nor turn back in your heart to Egypt again, nor ever hunger and thirst after the forbidden fruit again; so to Him that is able to keep you from falling, and to the word of his Grace (in your heart) I do commit and command you, the which as you keep to and learns of you will be enabled to persevere safely to the end, and in the end lie down in peace; and know the God of Peace to keep your heart and to keep your mind in peace; which is the blessed fruit and effect of righteousness, of well-doing, of faithfulness, diligence and watchfulness; the which as you are found in, grace and peace will be multiplied in you and to you, through the knowledge of God, and Jesus our Lord, who has called us to glory and virtue, to whom be praise for evermore.

W. S.

If this little book shall come into the hands of such who account themselves religious, and are zealous for the doctrines and traditions of their fore-fathers, and can say much for Christianity, God, Christ and the Holy Scriptures; but are highly offended and displeased, indeed, sometimes incensed and enraged against a little remnant of people that God has raised up in this age, to bear witness to the way of the Lord, under the name Light, Grace, Law, Spirit and Power of God within: and because they call and endeavor to persuade their neighbors and countrymen to come to walk therein; accounting it a new sort of doctrine, inconsistent with Christ and Christianity, giving it despicable names, and etcetera.

To such my earnest request is, (even in love and good-will to you) seeing that you say, you love, believe and honor the Scriptures; that you would show your selves like the Bereans, (who were called noble for so doing) with an unprejudiced mind to search the Scriptures, especially the following, quoted Chapter and Verse for your ease, be serious, take leisure to read them, meditate a little, laying aside your sensual thoughts, conceivings and imaginations, and that wisdom which is from beneath; which darkens the counsel of God, and wrested the scriptures, then you may clearly perceive that it is no new doctrine to preach the Light, nor error to assent that it is the way of God, that leads all that turn to it and walk in it, into true Christianity: so if any objection arises and remains in your mind concerning the way of God here born testimony to, if any words that can be read, written or spoken, are able to give you a satisfactory

To the Christian Reader

convincing answer thereto; the scriptures are those words, especially to you that professes an honor and obedience to them.

But this in short I testify to you, that if you sleight the gift of God, the manifestation of his Spirit, Light and Grace bestowed upon you, and given to you as one talent at least to improve; you can not understand nor receive the testimony of the scriptures, much less mine. So if you have any desire to understand the holy scriptures and other things of God; you must come to know and love the Light, Law and Spirit of God, and feel the operation of it in your own heart, to fit and prepare you to understand the divine mysteries of his Kingdom, and to inherit them; until which, though you may account yourself wise, rich and full, and are clothed with a profession of Christianity, yet you are poor, blind, miserable and naked, being covered with a covering, but not with the Spirit of the Lord; not with a meek and quiet Spirit; not with a Christ like Spirit; not with the Spirit of the primitive Christians.

So not in a capacity to understand their words, though you may profess them as the Jews did the Law and the Prophets, yet persecuted Him of whom they testified: That you may avoid doing the same, I counsel you to receive the Grace of God, the Light and Spirit of God, which appears in you, and shines to you, in order to lead you and guide you to everlasting life; and this is the will of God and his people; that all men might come to the knowledge of the Truth and be saved; not only from Hell, damnation and punishment; but from committing of sin the cause thereof.

And by this one thing, you may know whether your heart be right in the sight of the Lord, whether the Spirit and nature of Christianity be prevalent in you, yes or no, if you are not as much afraid to commit sin, as you are of Hell and punishment; if the doing of evil has not become so odious and hateful to you (because contrary to the nature and mind of God) that if there was no reward of Punishment entailed upon the doing thereof; yet you would not defile yourself therewith, nor dishonor your God, nor your profession of his Name; if it be not so with you, you has cause, yes great cause to question whether you are indeed what you have a Name, Profession or an Opinion to be, that is a Christian.

The Testimony of the Holy Scriptures
Concerning the LIGHT which is Spiritual.

Job 29:3. When his Candle shined upon my Head, and when by his Light I walked through Darkness.

Isa. 9: 2. The People that walked in Darkness, have seen a great Light: they that dwell in the Land of the shadow of Death, upon them hath the Light shined.

Isa. 60. I. Arise, shine; for thy Light is come, and the glory of the Lord is risen upon thee.

Luke 2: 32. A Light to lighten the Gentiles, and the glory of thy People Israel.

John 8: 12. Then spake Jesus again unto them, saying, I am the Light of the World: He that followeth me, shall not walk in Darkness, but shall have the Light of Life.

John 12: 36. While ye have Light, believe in the Light, that ye may be the Children of Light.

John 12: 46. I am come a Light into the World, that whosoever believeth on me, should not abide in Darkness.

2 Cor. 4: 6. For God who commanded the Light to shine out of Darkness, hath shined in our Hearts, to give the light of the knowledge of the glory of God, in the face of Jesus Christ.

Col. 1; 12. Giving thanks unto the Father, which hath made us meet to be partakers of the Inheritance of the Saints in Light.

2 Tim. 1: 10. But is now made manifest by the appearing of our Savior Jesus Christ, who hath abolished Death, and hath brought Life and Immortality to Light, through the Gospel.

1 John 1: 5. This then is the message which we have heard of him, and declare unto you, that God is Light, and in him is no Darkness at all.

1 John 1: 7. But if we walk in the Light as he is in the Light, we have fellowship one with another, and the Blood of Jesus Christ his Son cleanseth us from all Sin.

1 John 2: 8. Again, a new Commandment I write unto you, which thing is true in him and in you: because the Darkness is past, and the true Light now shineth.

1 John 2: 9. He that saith he is in the Light, and hateth his Brother, is in Darkness even until now.

1 John 2: 10. He that loveth his Brother abideth in the Light, and there is none occasion of stumbling in him.

2 Peter 1: 19. We have also a more sure word of Prophecy, whereunto ye do well than ye take heed, as unto a Light that shineth in a dark place, until the Day dawn, and the day-star arise in your Hearts.

The Holy Scriptures

1 Peter 2: 9. But ye are a chosen Generation, a royal Priesthood, an holy Nation, a peculiar People; that ye should shew forth the praises of him, who hath called you out of Darkness into his marvelous Light.

Rev. 21: 24. And the Nations of them that are saved, shall walk in the Light of it; and the Kings of the Earth, do bring their glory and honor into it,

1 Thess. 5: 5. Ye are all the Children of Light, and the Children of the Day: we are not of the Night, nor of Darkness.

Eph. 5: 8. For ye were sometimes Darkness, but now are ye Light in the Lord: walk as Children of Light.

Eph. 5: 13. But all things that are reproved are made manifest by the Light: for whatsoever doth make manifest, is Light.

Isa. 2: 5. O House of Jacob, come ye, and let us walk in the Light of the Lord.

Ps. 27: 1. The Lord is my Light, and my Salvation; whom shall I fear? the Lord is the strength of my Life; of whom shall I be afraid?

Ps. 119: 105. Thy word is a Lamp unto my feet, and a Light unto my path.

Mic. 7: 8. Rejoice not against me, O mine Enemy: when I fall, I shall arise; when I sit in Darkness, the Lord shall be a Light unto me.

John 1: 4. In him was Life, and the Life was the Light of Men.

John 1: 5. And the Light shineth in Darkness, and the Darkness comprehended it not.

John 1: 7. The same came for witness, to bear witness of the Light, that all Men through him might believe.

John 1: 8. He was not that Light, but was sent to bear witness of that Light.

John 1: 9. That was the true Light, which lighteth every Man that cometh into the World.

John 3: 10. And this is the Condemnation, that Light is come into the World, and Men loved Darkness rather then Light, because their deeds were Evil.

John 3: 20. For every one that doth Evil hateth the Light, neither cometh to the Light, lest his deeds should be reproved.

John 3: 21. But he that doth the Truth, cometh to the Light, that his deeds may be made manifest, that they are wrought in God.

Acts 13: 47. For so has the Lord commanded us, saying, I have set thee to be a Light of the Gentiles, that thou shouldest be for Salvation unto the ends of the Earth.

Acts 26: 18. To open their Eyes, and to turn them from Darkness to Light, and from the power of Satan unto God, that they may receive forgiveness of Sins, and inheritance among them which are sanctified by faith that is in me.

Acts 23: That Christ should suffer, and that he should be the first that should rise from the Dead, and should shew Light unto the People, and to the Gentiles.

The Holy Scriptures

The Testimony of the Holy Scriptures concerning the LAW, SPIRIT, WORD, GRACE, LOVE, and POWER of GOD Within.

Ps. 37: 31. The Law of his God is in his heart, none of his steps shall slide.

Ps. 40: 8. I delight to do thy Will, O my God: yea, thy Law is within my Heart.

Isa. 51: 7. Hearken unto me, ye that know Righteousness, the People in whose Heart is my Law; fear ye not the reproach of Men, neither be ye afraid of their revilings.

Rom. 2: 14. For when the Gentiles which have not the Law, do by nature the things contained in the Law, these having not the Law, are a Law unto themselves:

Rom. 2: 15. Which shew the work of the Law written in their Hearts, their Conscience also bearing witness, and their Thoughts the mean while accusing, or else excusing one another.

Rom. 8: 2. For the Law of the Sprit of Life in Christ Jesus, has made me free from the Law of Sin and Death.

Rom. 8: 9. But ye are not in the Flesh, but in the Spirit, if so be that the Spirit of God dwell in you. Now if any Man have not the Spirit of Christ, he is none of his.

Rom. 8: 10. And if Christ be in you, the Body is dead because of Sin, but the Spirit is Life, because of Righteousness,

Rom. 8: 11. But if the Spirit of him that raised up Jesus from the Dead, dwell in you; he that raised up Christ from the Dead, shall also quicken your Mortal Bodies, by his Spirit that dwelleth in you.

Rom. 8: 13. For if ye live after the Flesh, ye shall Die: but if ye through the Spirit do mortify the deeds of the Body, ye shall Live.

Rom. 8: 16. The Spirit itself beareth witness with our Spirit, that we are the Children of God.

Rom. 8: 23. And not only they but our selves also which have the first-fruits of the Spirit, even we our selves groan within our selves, waiting for the Adoption, to wit the Redemption of our Body.

Rom. 8: 26. Likewise the Spirit also helpeth our Infirmities: for we know not what we should pray for as we ought: but the Spirit itself maketh intercession for us with groanings which cannot be uttered.

1 Cor. 12: 7. But the manifestation of the Spirit, is given to every Man to profit withall.

1 Cor. 2: 4. And my Speech, and my Preaching was not with enticing words of Mans Wisdom, but in demonstration of the Spirit, and of Power.

The Holy Scriptures

1 Cor. 2: 10. But God has revealed them unto us by his Spirit: for the Spirit searcheth all things, yea, the deep things of God.

1 Cor. 2.: 11. For what Man knoweth the things of a Man, save the Spirit of Man which is in him? Even so the things of God knoweth no Man, but the Spirit of God.

1 Cor. 2: 12. Now we have received, not the Spirit of the World, but the Spirit which is of God; that we might know the things that are freely given to us of God.

1 Cor. 6: 17. But he that is joined unto the Lord is one Spirit.

1 John 3: 24. And he that keepeth his Commandments, dwelleth in him, and he in him: and hereby we know that he abideth in us, by the Spirit which he hath given us.

1 John 4.:13. Hereby know we that we dwell in him, and he in us, because he hath given us of his Spirit.

1 Peter 1: 11. Searching what, or what manner of time the Spirit of Christ which was in them did signify, when it testified before-hand the suffering, of Christ, and the glory that should follow.

2 Tim. 1: 7. For God has not given us the Spirit of Fear, but of Power, of Love, and of a sound Mind.

Gal. 4: 6. And because ye are Sons, God has sent forth the Spirit of his Son into your Hearts, Crying, Abba, Father.

Gal. 5: 16. This I say then, Walk in the Spirit, and ye shall not fulfil the Lust of the Flesh.

Gal. 5: 25. If we Live in the Spirit, let us also Walk in the Spirit.

Ephes. 2; 22. In whom you also are builded together for an Habitation of God through the Spirit.

Ephes. 3: 20. Now unto him that is able to do exceeding abundantly above all that we ask or think, according to the Power that worketh in us,

John 5: 38. And ye have not his Word abiding in you: for whom he has sent, him ye believe not.

John 5: 42. But I know you, that you have not the Love of God in you.

John 6: 53. Then Jesus said unto him, Verily, verily I say unto you, Except ye eat the Flesh of the Son of Man, and drink his Blood, ye have no Life in you.

John 8: 37. I know that ye are Abraham's seed, but ye seek to kill me, because my Word has no place in you.

John 14: 17. Even the Spirit of Truth, whom the World cannot receive, because it seeth him not, neither knoweth him: but ye know him, for he dwelleth with you, and shall be in you.

John 15: 4. Abide in me, and I in you: as the Branch cannot bear fruit of itself, except it abide in the Vine; no more can ye, except ye abide in me.

The Holy Scriptures

John 15: 7. If ye abide in me, and my Words abide in you, ye shall ask what ye will, and it shall be done unto you.

Rom. 8: 10. And if Christ be in you, the Body is Dead because of Sin: but the Spirit is Life because of Righteousness.

Rom. 8: 11. But if the Spirit of him that raised up Jesus from the Dead, dwell in you: he that raised up Christ from the Dead shall also quicken your Mortal Bodies, by his Spirit that dwelleth in you.

1 Cor. 3: 16. Know ye not that ye are the Temple of God; and that the Spirit of God dwelleth in you.

1 Cor. 6: 19. What, know you not that your Body is the Temple of the Holy Ghost which is in you, which ye have of God, and ye are not your own?

1 Cor. 14: 25. And thus are the secrets of his Heart made manifest, and so falling down on his Face, he will Worship God, and report that God is in you of a truth.

2 Cor. 13: 5. Examine your souls whether ye be in the Faith: prove your own selves; know ye not your own selves, how that Jesus Christ is in you, except ye be Reprobates?

Gal. 4: 15. Where is then the Blessedness you speak of? for I bear you record, that if it had been possible, ye would have plucked out your own Eyes, and have given them unto me.

Ephes. 4: 6. One God and Father of all, who is above all, and through all, and in you all.

Phil. 2: 5. Let this Mind be in you, which was also in Christ Jesus.

Phil. 13. For it is God which worketh in you, both to will and to do of his good pleasure.

Col. 1: 27. To whom God would make known what is the riches of the glory of this mystery among the Gentiles, which is Christ in you the hope of glory.

Col.3,:16. Let the Word of Christ dwell in you richly in all Wisdom, teaching and admonishing one another in Psalms, and Hymns, and Spiritual Songs, singing with grace in your Hearts to the Lord.

2 Thess. 1: 12. That the Name of our Lord Jesus Christ may be glorified in you, and ye in him, according to the Grace of our God, and the Lord Jesus Christ.

1 John 2: 14. I have written unto you, Fathers, because ye have known him that is from the beginning. I have written unto you Young Men, because ye are strong, and the Word of God abideth in you, and ye have overcome the Wicked One.

1 John 2: 27. But the anointing which ye have received of him, abideth in you: and ye need not that any man teach you: but as the same anointing teacheth you of all things, and is truth and is no lye: and even as it has taught you, ye shall abide in him.

1 John 4: 4. Ye are of God, little Children, and have overcome them: because greater is he that is in you, then he that is in the World.

The Holy Scriptures

1 John 3.:3. And every man that has this Hope in him, purifieth himself even as he is pure.

1 John 3: 15. Whosoever hateth his Brother, is a Murderer, and he know that no Murderer hath eternal Life abiding in him.

1 John 4: 13. Hereby know we that we dwell in him, and he in us, because he hath given us of his Spirit.

1 John 4.:15. Whosoever shall confess that Jesus is the Son of God, God dwelleth in him, and he in God.

1 John 4: 16. And we have known, and believed that Love that God hath to us. God is Love, and he that dwelleth in Love, dwelleth in God, and God in him.

1 John 5: 20. And we know that the Son of God is come, and hath given us an understanding that we may know him that is true: and we art in him that is true, specifically in his Son Jesus Christ. This is the true God, and eternal Life.

So you may perceive and understand by these scriptures, that the righteous men and Christians in ages past were witnesses of the Light of God shining in them, and to them, of the Word, Law, Power, Grace and Love of God manifesting, appearing and operating in them; the which if you are ignorant of, and a stranger to, you can neither be a righteous man nor a Christian, profess what you will.

Many who profess God, Christ and Christianity, are grown into such gross sensuality, that to speak or write to them of the spiritual appearance and work of God, in and by his Light, Law, Grace, Spirit, and etcetera, and the powerful operation thereof within, upon the mind, will, understanding, heart and conscience, seems so strange, so new, so incredible, that they can in no way give any regard unto it, but rather mock and deride thereat, as if they had never seen nor read the Holy Scriptures; whose testimony thereto is as clear as the morning without clouds; which is an evident sign and demonstration that their eyes are closed, their hearts and ears are hardened and dull of hearing, their understandings dark, and their minds so sensual, that they are become dead; for to be sensually minded is death.

And in this death the sensual-minded man can talk of the fame of wisdom; but possess and inherit folly, and lie down in sorrow, whose state and condition is much pitied and lamented by a little Remnant, who are ready to say in love and good-will to their neighbors and countrymen, come here and we will tell you what the Lord has done for our souls, which were as yours are, in death and darkness, in bondage and captivity, even while professors of other things: and this is the end of every true Christian in writing, printing, preaching, and so on, that is that people might come to have the eye of their understanding opened, and know the Day-Star to arise in their hearts, that they may see their way out of death and darkness, ignorance and sensuality; and receive the Light of Life, and therein wisdom to understand and receive the sayings of Holy Men recorded in the Holy Scriptures; until which they will wrest them to their own destruction, and never truly understand nor receive the comfort of them; nor of any words proceeding from the same Spirit of God in this age: this is the word of Truth to all it may concern, which together with the scriptures I have quoted; I intend shall serve for an answer to all objections that shall be made by the nominal Christian or bare professor of Christ and Christianity, into whose hand this little book may come, knowing assuredly that there is no end of contending with such with pen, ink and paper: but however I can in Truth subscribe myself their Friend.

W.S.

Some Reasons why the Holy Scriptures are to be Esteemed and Preferred, by the True Christians, ABOVE Other Writings, (though from the same Spirit) in this Generation.

First, because they give an account of the diverse dispensations and operations of God before and after the Fall, in order to lead mankind out of the Fall, and to restore him into his primitive estate again; the manner, method and order of which is in the depth of the Wisdom of God, declared and set forth in the Holy Scriptures, to the man of God, more than in any other book whatsoever.

Secondly. Because therein are recorded the diverse sayings, testimonies and experiences of many righteous men, throughout all those various dispensations and appearances and operations of God before the Law, under the Law and Prophets, and also under the Gospel; being all briefly and plainly set forth to the man of God, for the increase of his learning, encouragement of his hope, strengthening of his faith, and confirming of his confidence.

Thirdly. Because the nominal Christian pretends he has a great esteem for the scriptures, and cries them up for his only rule, to walk and order his conversation by; so that the true Christian, and minister of Christianity has a great advantage thereby, in order to reprove, persuade and convince the nominal Christian that he does not obey, nor walks according to his own professed rule.

Fourthly. Because it is the custom, nature and practice of the spirit of darkness, deceit and persecution; to despise, sleight and condemn righteous men, their words and writings while they live; and to garnish their sepulchers, and profess honor to them when they are dead; so though it be but in words, (that they advance them above themselves as their rule and guide) they are of great service to the true Christian and minister of Christianity; for the detection and conviction of gainsayers; and vindication of his doctrine and practice, life and conversation; therefore to be esteemed above other writings, they being in some sort as a wall of defense to him.

Fifthly. Because the general good and Salvation of all mankind is the principal aim and end of the true Christian, and Christian minister; and seeing in this part of the world called Christendom, they profess a great reverence and esteem to the sayings and writings of Holy Men in generations of old; not much regarding what is written by the same Spirit in Holy Men in the present age, though one with the scriptures: as Christ convinced the Jews out of the Law and the Prophets; Paul the Athenians out of their own poets sayings, which were of esteem among them; So the true Christian and minister of Christ who has unity with the scripture, and with the Holy Men's spirits that gave them forth, has the same advantage now against those that only profess them in words and live not the Life they exhort to and call for. So for this reason good cause to value them above other books though written by the same spirit in this age; specifically that those people who want the Salvation the scriptures bear witness of, might come to be made wise through faith to Salvation by them.

COUNSEL
TO THE
Christian-Traveller.

Put your hand to the plow (look not back) keep it there until the fallow ground be plowed up, and the briars and thorns rooted up and destroyed, so that the seed may grow up in you to perfection.

Have you known the kingdom and the power, in which it stands, like a little leaven hid in the three measures of Meal? Hinder not its working; let it leaven the whole lump?

Do you know the field where the pearl of great price is hidden? Then dig deep, and find it; and when you have found it, sell all, and purchase it, and then you will be the wise Merchantman indeed.

Have you traveled out of Egypt, through the Red Sea, and wilderness? And have you known the right arm of the Lord accompanying you, and supporting you in your trials, temptations and besetments that you have met with therein? Keep still to the same arm and power that has called, lead and sustained you hitherto, and it will bring you into the promised land, and not only so, but he will give you a possession therein, and destroy your enemies, that did possess it; and you will have a house given you, you did not build; and a vineyard, you did not plant; and a well, you did not dig; and it shall spring up in you to everlasting life, and you shall sit under your own vine, and under your own fig-tree, and lie down where none can make you afraid; you shall be blessed in your basket and in your store, in your going out and coming in, lying down and rising up, these blessings shall assuredly attend you, as you love the day of small things, and are faithful in following the Lord, who has appeared by his Light and grace to you, for your perfect redemption, restoration, and everlasting Salvation.

I say, you will certainly enjoy and inherit these things, and receive nor only the addition of virtue, knowledge, temperance, patience, and so on to your faith, but also the very end of your faith; for faith and hope has an end, and it is a blessed thing to receive the end thereof, specifically Salvation; and there is only those who endure to the end that can be saved; specifically to the end of the work of God, of the new creation of God in Christ Jesus.

Many may begin well, and make a good progress also, and yet fall short; they may know the first days work, read Gen. 1. The Spirit of God moving upon the face of the waters, the appearance of the light, and the division of light from darkness, and to call the light day, and the darkness night, which is more than all that the wise, prudent, religious men of this world can know or do; who are all as the waters, and the whore sits upon them, and the moving of the Spirit of God thereon that they despise and disregard, the appearance of light they hate, so that it shines in darkness, and is not divided, and the darkness cannot comprehend it, so that it cannot give true names to things, cannot call the light, day, nor the darkness, night, but err and mistake so far, as to call the light, darkness, and the darkness, light. It is this that all men in the fall are prone to, and found doing, under the old heavens, and upon the old earth; this is as a note by the way to those it does concern.

But in order to proceed, they must also know the 2nd and 3rd days work, The firmament in the midst of the waters, the waters divided, and the dry land appearing, and bringing forth seed and fruit after its kind, which is good; this is more than words, names and profession, these have some standing, some foundation in the midst of the waters, these are as trees that bear fruit, and the earth yields its increase to him that cultivates it.

And the 4th day it is written, God made two great lights, the one to rule the day, and the other to rule the night; the light and the rule and government thereof, must be witnessed and known also; and as in the 5th days work there must be a bringing forth and multiplying abundantly, and a flying above the earth, in the open firmament of heaven; and the 6th days work will be known, to be made in the likeness and image of God, blessed and endued with heavenly power and dominion over all; placed in a garden planted by the Lord; a restoration into innocence and uprightness by Christ that the power, light, love, and wisdom of God will be attained to, and arrived at; yet eve in this very estate there is danger. There is a sort of proneness to look out at the beauty of the works of God, and to feed upon them, and delight yourself with them, or to eat that which is forbidden, unless the Law and Command of God are kept close to and obeyed. The Sun that's placed in the midst of the works of God must rule the day, and the children of it; and the Moon the night. He that has wisdom let him understand; the voice of the serpent must not be listened to. If you will keep your habitation, and preserve your dwelling place in Paradise, in the garden of God, you must cultivate it, and care for it. Likewise take care of your heart with all diligence: if any thing appears therein that would entice and allure you, counsel and persuade you to break the Law of God; see to it that you consent not, see that you do it not, but abide in the rule and dominion that God has given you (not only over the serpent, but) over all the works of his hands; and in so doing you will know and understand the reason of the godly jealousy and fear of the Apostle, who said to such as were brought to a good estate, (specifically espoused to one husband, in order to be presented as a chaste virgin to Christ: (which is a state very near the marriage union) 2 Cor. 11:2-3. I fear (said he) lest by any means, as the serpent deceived Eve through his subtlety, so your minds should be corrupted from the simplicity that is in Christ. It is you that have been espoused and adorned as a bride for her husband; until you have come to the simplicity that is in Christ; and it is you that has escaped the corruption that is in the world through lust; it is you that have been restored, redeemed and brought back again into innocence, and has a place in the garden of God, that the serpent would again betray, deceive and overthrow. Therefore keep in your dominion, power, and wisdom, which God has endued you with, that he has armed you and surrounded you with; and the serpent shall never prevail against you. Look not at the first Adam in any other way than to take warning by him, lest you act like him and receive the same reward. But look at Christ, the second Adam, in whom the serpent, the deceiver, the devil has no part, (though he has power to tempt in Paradise, and to make war in heaven, and appear before the Lord and accuse,) neither could he ever deceive, overcome or prevail against Christ, neither can he against you, as you keep close to Christ, armed with his power, and your mind staid upon God your Savior. This will bring you into a surer estate then the first Adam was in, and for a time enjoyed in Paradise; so that you may come to be not only taken and put into the garden of God to cultivate it and to care for it; but that you may also be brought to have a place in his house, in the Temple of God, and be as a pillar therein, and go never leave; so that you may become like Mount Zion, which cannot be moved, so that your heart may be established with grace, settled, grounded, and fixed upon the rock that is higher than you, against whom the wiles, devices, subtle bates and allurements on the one hand, nor storms and tempests of the enemy on the other hand can prevail. For you will come to see eye to eye, and know as you are known, you will come to know the Lord, as one, and his Name, as one, (not many names) the first to the last and the last to be first; the beginning the end, and the end the beginning; and your heavenly rest with him, who is without beginning or end, to whom be praise for evermore. And this is the end, yes, the blessed end of the work of God, that all are to know made and accomplished in themselves, by Christ the Light, Power, and Wisdom of God: but on the way to this end there is great danger, as you that have been and are a traveler therein know right well; and there are many things written for your comfort and for your learning in the Holy Scriptures, which I would have you esteem and account a great mercy that you have the use and benefit of them, of whom it is said by Paul to Timothy, Tim. 3. 15, 16, 17. They are able to make wise to Salvation through faith in Christ Jesus; who is indeed the wisdom of God, the opener of the scriptures, the only leader into the true understanding of them; and it is by and through faith in him that the man of God comes to be made perfect, and thoroughly furnished to all good works; and it is the man of God only that has the comfort of the scriptures, and that has unity and fellowship with the Holy Men's spirits that wrote them, or gave them forth; and it is he alone that understands them; they are as a sealed book to the learned and unlearned, to the professor or nominal Christian and profane. Great is the mystery of godliness which is revealed and revealing to babes, and hidden from the strong men, from the wise and prudent School-men of this world, who make a career out of the history of godliness for the sake of money; to the destruction of their own souls and the souls of others.

Now tender Friend, that you may persevere safely in your way, always remember the counsel of Christ Jesus, take heed or pray that your flight be not in the winter, nor upon the Sabbath day: these two seasons are most dangerous; there is much in the words; the wisdom of God spoke them; and it is those that are endowed with the same only that can understand them; and by the same you may be preserved in the winter, and through the winter, and be able to say, the winter is past, and the summer is come, and the singing of birds is heard in your land; and also know the Lord of the Sabbath, and to rest in him; who has been and is the dwelling place of his people in all ages and generations; to whom be glory for ever and evermore.

Thus I have briefly touched and shown how the inward work or new creation of God, holds parallel with the history of the outward or old creation, and what danger attends you when you are a plant of God, specifically in Paradise itself, which man lost through disobedience and transgression?

I have it also in my mind briefly to set before you, the method and order of the wisdom of God in your restoration, in the work of Salvation; and the danger that attends in the way thereto typified and shadowed forth, by, and in the history of his people, being oppressed in the land of Egypt; and their cries to him, and his coming down to deliver them, and his raising them a captain or leader, and his bringing them out with a strong hand, and leading them through the Red Sea, and destroying their enemies therein, and bringing them to the banks on the other side, and his giving them a Song of Deliverance and Salvation, and leading them through the wilderness, feeding them with manna and quails from heaven, and water out of the rock, going before them in a Pillar of Fire by night, and a Pillar of Cloud by day, bringing them to Mount Sinai, and giving them his law, statues, and judgments, prepared his Ark, and reared up his Tabernacle, and fastened the sockets, set up the boards, and put in the bars thereof, and reared up his pillars, and brought the Ark of the Testimony into the Tabernacle, set bread in order upon the table, the lamps lighted, sweet incense offered upon the golden altar, and the glory of the Lord appeared in the Tabernacle, and was their guide in all their journeys. This was glorious in its time, and the anti-type or thing signified thereby the traveling Christian only knows and understands; these were great helps, great benefits and blessings, accompanying them in the way to the Promised Land.

Yet consider, that notwithstanding all these things, and all their experiences of the outstretched hand, power, and presence of the Lord, his promises to the obedient, and his threatening to the rebellious and disobedient, yet they forgot the Lord, turned back in their hearts, and so through unbelief, murmuring and disobedience fell by the way, and never entered into the rest, into the Promised Land, which flowed with milk and honey, all miscarried and came short, that came out of Egypt, through the Red Sea, and so on above twenty years old, except Joshua and Caleb, and then when their off-spring came to possess and inhabit Canaan, the Promised Land, consider how in the process of time they corrupted themselves, and grieved the spirit of the Lord to that degree through their backslidings, and abominations, (not only before but also after God had erected his Temple, and furnished it in a most magnificent manner, with vessels of gold, silver, and brass, and other costly ornaments, and holiness to the Lord written thereon, and his own presence and glorious appearance therein, yet after all this) that through sin and disobedience all became a prey to the spoiler, and themselves made captive, and carried away into a strange land.

These things are written for the learning and warning of the wise in heart, whose eye God has opened, and to whom he has revealed his arm of power, and done many wondrous works in them and for them, that they turn not again into folly, into carelessness, into wantonness, into pride and rebellion against the Spirit of God, that they deck not themselves with Gods jewels, and play the harlot with them, as they did, and so receive the same reward in the mystery as they did in the history; of which there is as great danger now in the inward, as there was then in the outward; for likewise in the dispensation of the spirit in the end of the prophets, I may also hint at the work of God therein, and show that the same danger attends mankind in the way thereof, the mystery of godliness is great, and the mystery of iniquity is great also, and happy are you if you abide in the Light of God, which makes them both manifest. It is not enough to know the Light to shine, but to walk and abide in it, and be a true child of it. It is not enough to know the Spirit of Truth and the power of it, but to be led by it and joined to it, and become one with it, and to bring forth the fruit thereof. It is not enough to know the seed of the kingdom and the sowing of it, but its springing up, and breaking thorough the clods, and growing up, not only into the stalk and blade, but into the full ear and corn; and not only so, but to be reaped and gathered into the garner, for the use of the Lord of the Harvest. It is not enough to know one of the days of the Son of Man, the child born, and the son given; but the government upon His shoulders, His reigning in your heart, His and your enemies destroyed, and to attain thereto according to the phrase used in the Holy Scriptures. There is an overshadowing of the Holy Ghost to be known, a begetting and forming Christ within to be known, and a traveling to bring forth, and a being born, and a growing up from one stature to another, from a child to a young man, from a young man to an elder, and a suffering with Christ; a taking up his Cross daily and following him, a dying with him, and a rising with him, and a seeking those things which are above, where Christ sits at the right hand of God; you must be risen with Christ before you are in a capacity to seek those things that are at the right hand of God; but it is a farther estate to find them, and to be seated in a heavenly place in Christ Jesus; and to sit down in the Kingdom with Abraham, Isaac, and Jacob, and the furthest and greatest state of all, is to know the Kingdom delivered up to the Father, and God become all in all; where that alone safety is, until which (though you are a disciple of Christ, and become as a chaste wife virgin espoused to him) you must watch and pray, and care for your lamp trimmed, your light burning, lest you enter into temptation, lest you slumber and sleep, and the door be shut against you; for there is a possibility, yes, a real danger of loss in all estates and growths, until you get into Abraham's bosom: there the gulf is known to be fixed; there is no changing states then, as is signified in the parable of Dives[the rich man] and Lazarus, Luke 16. Between us and you there is a great gulf fixed, so that they that would pass from us to you cannot, neither can they pass to us that would come from thence: and to speak a little according to this parabolic discourse between Abraham and Dives [the rich man], they that would go to Hell cannot, and they that would go to Heaven cannot, the one can do nothing against the Truth, he is so governed by it, he is so in love and unity with it; the other can do nothing for the truth, he is so in enmity and hardness of heart against it, having lost his day of visitation is become sealed up in darkness, in a sense of his loss; for this greatly adds to the torments of the wicked, to lift up their eyes in Hell, and to see and behold the state of the righteous afar off, and themselves in a state of torment and misery, crying and praying for mercy and relief, and cannot be heard nor eased of their pain, the sun being set upon them, and their day being turned into utter darkness, and is also become their dwelling or habitation, where the weeping, wailing, and gnashing of teeth is.

So dear Friend, you may perceive by what I have briefly hinted, and by the current of the Holy Scriptures, and by your own experience, that it is no easy thing to be a true Christian, it is no easy thing to go through the work of regeneration of the new creation of God in Christ Jesus. It is no easy thing to travail to the end of your journey, and to go through the warfare, and to be able to say with the Apostle, I have fought a good fight, I have finished my course, henceforth is a crown of glory laid up for me, and to come to the wearing of the crown, and to be more than a conqueror in him that has loved you.

These things to witness and enjoy is the blessed end of all the dispensations of God since the fall; and he that is the conqueror, the over-comer, and is more than a conqueror, he has certainly received the white stone, wherein the new name is written, which none know but he that has it; he is the wise merchant man, that has sold all and purchased the pearl of great price, which over-values all things besides; he has right to eat of the tree of life, which grows in the midst of the garden; he is blessed with all spiritual blessings, in heavenly places in Christ Jesus; he is a co-heir, a joint-heir with Him; and not only so, but he is come into his inheritance into possession, this is his state, though he may meet with no better entertainment in the world, than Christ the captain of his Salvation, (his elder brother) and disciples did.

So it is your enjoying the light of God's countenance, it is your being joined to the Lord, and being become one Spirit with him; it is your knowing the marriage union, your maker to be your husband, that is your comfort, your joy and rejoicing; your crown and diadem in prosperity and in adversity; in heights and in depths; in the palace and in the dungeon; in all states, times, and places; you are the only happy man that are partaker of these things, though your goods may be spoiled, and your body in the hands of your enemies, yet you can really seal to the truth of that testimony of Paul in his Epistle to the Romans; when he said, I reckon that the sufferings of this present time, are not worthy to be compared to the glory that shall be revealed in us; and to you this time of revelation has come, you know the Lord has come, and His reward is with Him a Hundred-fold; specifically in this time, and in the World to come life everlasting; godliness with content is great gain, it has the promises of all good present and to come; and they that have resigned up themselves, and all into the hand of God; has nothing to lose, has nothing to take care for, but to please the Lord; and it is the food and drink of such to do His will, and His paths are all paths of pleasantness; there is no bitterness in the later end of such as walk therein.

So in your way consider and be warned, by the examples recorded in the Holy Scriptures, and always remember that they tell you of a people that come to the knowledge of God his law, statutes, and ordinances, and manner of worship which he himself commanded, which while performed in the sincerity of heart (though but shadowy and typical) he was well pleased with, and his blessings and presence accompanied them; but when they lost the sincerity, uprightness, and integrity of heart: though they kept in the exact practice, and performance of the outward part of worship; yet all their doing and performances were abomination to him, and rejected by him, as is testified by his Prophet Isaiah, saying, he that killed an ox, is as if he slew a man; he that sacrificed a Lamb, is as if he cut off a dogs neck; he that offered an oblation, is if he offered swine's blood; he that burned incense, as if he blessed an idol. This is mighty strange to those that know not the real cause of it, that those doings and services commanded should become so hateful, odious, and abominable in the sight of Him that commanded them; God looks at the heart, at the inside, if that be gone astray, if that be corrupted, degenerated and fallen in love with the creatures; He accepts of nothing as well done from man in this estate, his righteousness and his wickedness are both abomination to him: this was a harsh evil the people fell into under the dispensation of the law, they kept sinning and sacrificing, but neglected to hear and obey the Voice of the Lord. Likewise in the dispensation of the Gospel, specifically in the first ages of it, the like evil was creeping in. By the preaching of the Apostles many were brought to believe in Christ, and to make profession of him, and it soon grew to this pass with some that they were ready to sit down, or rest in the profession and knowledge of Christ after the flesh; and to observe the form of godliness, but deny and neglect the power.

The ministers of Christ in the primitive times had a great work before them.

First, to persuade and convince the Jews that Jesus was the Christ of God, the Messiah promised and prophesied of by the holy prophets; (whom they persecuted and slew in one age, and honored at least with their lips, and garnished their sepulchers in another.)

Secondly, to oppose their Temple worship, shadowy and typical ordinances and observances, which God once commanded; and to bring them from under them to the thing signified by them, and to believe in Him who was the end and substance thereof, who did fulfill all righteousness continued in the law, in the prophets and John; then when they had brought people to believe that Christ was the great prophet, which God promised to raise up like to Moses, how ready were many of these believers to sit down in this belief, and to content themselves with a knowledge of Christ after the flesh; like as the Jews pleased themselves with the Temple of the Lord, and with their outward observances, while they lacked the root of the matter, namely an upright, broken, contrite heart, which is and was the only sacrifice God delighted in; so that they were constrained to testify against the bare knowledge of Christ after the flesh, and as it were pass it by, Paul saying, henceforth we know no man after the flesh; indeed, though we have known Christ after the Flesh, we know Him so no more; pressing the knowledge of Him after the Spirit, revealed, manifested and known by the work and operation of His Power and Spirit within; in whom this knowledge was lacking, they were reprobates. It was not enough to know Him born of the virgin, and to increase in wisdom and stature, and in favor with God and men, do many outward miracles, preach many excellent sermons, give forth many divine and heavenly precepts, go up and down doing good, suffering by, for, and because of sin and sinners, dying, rising and ascending into the glory of His Father. It was not sufficient to know and believe the history and truth of these things, in the primitive times, neither is it now; but you must also know and experience Him in His Spiritual appearance, power, and operation inwardly; and persevere therein, to the end of the work thereof, without which you will be as formal a Christian under the profession of Christ, and as much rejected in the account of God as the outward Jew was, when he kept in the outward practice and form of religion; and cried up the Temple of the Lord and its holiness outwardly, while he himself was a Temple of unholiness, uncleanness, and corruption.

Counsel to the Christian-Traveller

So dear Friend and fellow traveler, that we may run to the end of our race, and be certain of the crown; that we may fight not as those that beat the air, but as those that go on conquering and to conquer, keeping under all that would hinder us from running well to the end, and that would deprive us of the crown; and betray us into the hand of our enemies. I say, that we do this, let us always remember the sayings of the Apostle Paul, who was a wise experienced traveler, and an able minister of the covenant, 1 Corinthians: 9. I so run, not as uncertainly; I so fight, not as one that beats the air: but I keep under my body, and bring it into subjection, lest that by any means when I have preached to others I myself become a castaway; and in the 10th Chapter he gives an instance of the Jews, who were baptized into Moses in the cloud, and in the sea, and ate of the spiritual food, and drank of the spiritual drink, specifically of the spiritual rock that followed them, which rock was Christ, yet were overthrown in the wilderness, and destroyed of the destroyer; because when they did eat and drink, they rose up to play, and lusted after evil things; no (said he) these things happened to them for examples, and they are written for our admonition or learning, upon whom the ends of the world are come; wherefore let him that thinks he stands, take heed lest he fall. From which sayings with our own experience, we may observe and conclude, that it is the duty of teachers and preachers, hearers and learners, eaters and drinkers, specifically in the spiritual dispensation to take heed that they run well to the end; that they fight well to the end, that they eat and drink worthily; lest judgment overtake them while the food is in their mouths; even as it has some in this generation of ours, who after they knew God, did not glorify Him as God, but became vain in their imaginations, and their foolish hearts have deceived them to that degree, that under the very form and profession of Christ in His Spiritual appearance and work in the inward parts; they oppose and resist the thing itself both in themselves and others, and the mist and mystery of iniquity has so wrought in them, that they cannot see nor understand the same. This harsh evil all shall certainly escape, who make it their daily practice to walk in the fear of the Lord; and to keep their minds exercised in His law, meditating upon His mercies and judgments, new and old, past and present; so doing, no evil can prevail nor overtake such unawares.

So dear Friend and reader, whose good in writing I chiefly aim at, I desire you to be weighty and serious in reading, as I have been in writing; and you will find the benefit and comfort thereof, as I have done, ministered into your own bosom, and you will not only clearly perceive and understand the difference between the light, careless, overly reading, hearing, professing and talking of good things; and the serious weighty possession and enjoyment of them; but also between the beginning, progress, middle, and end of the work of God in the new creation, restoration, regeneration, and Salvation.

Counsel to the Christian-Traveller

So to the grace of God which leads to glory, and from one glory to another, I do heartily commend you; which grace is able and sufficient to teach you all good, and preserve you from all evil, and in the same I rest and remain your Friend and brother,

W.S.

Meditations & Experiences

I. It is a precious thing to know *what the cross of Christ is, and how to take it up, and make use of it;* for indeed, it is no less than the *Power that crucifies sin, and saves from it*; which *Christendom*, too generally being ignorant of, set up something else instead thereof, and so sin remains alive, uncrucified, and salvation is lacking; for it is not all the gold, silver, and wooden crosses, nor voluntary humility, in the whole world, that are able to crucify one sin, as to the nature of it, nor to make any one disciple, nor enable to watch with Christ one hour, nor follow Him one step in the regeneration.

II. It is a blessed state, to know the eye of the mind, not only opening, but, opened; thereby is ability and wisdom witnessed to read in the book of life, wherein all the treasures of wisdom and knowledge are hid; and he or she that knows this light shining, this eye opened in them, walks and stumbles not. This eye and light within, is that which Christendom too much despises and rejects, therefore walks in darkness and stumbles, and knows not whither they go. While we ourselves did so, we were darkness, walked in it, and our feet stumbled upon the dark mountains.

That which shut and stopped this eye, and darkened this light within, in the beginning, was sin and transgression, whereby mankind lost the sight and enjoyment of their Creator. And this I testify that no people upon the face of the Earth, come to witness this *eye of the mind* opened again, but as they come to experience that Power in themselves which crucifies sin, and saves and redeems out of transgression, and are also obedient and subject to it.

III. The remembrance of the *first day's work* is very precious, specifically the separation of the light from the darkness within, whereby we came to know each, its name and nature, and to have our minds turned from the darkness *within*, to the light *within*; from the power of Satan *within*, to the Power of God *within*; from the teachers and books *without*, to the graced, the anointing, the true teacher *within*. The remembrance of this is very precious: and now what remains, but that we walk in this light, that we may be children of it indeed, and that we be always obedient to this Power, and learn of this anointing, until we are fully educated. It is the substance of all; it is the end of all words and writings; indeed, it is the end of all the dispensations of God, since the beginning.

IV. The precious light that shines in the heart, is the *everlasting Day of God*, in which He walks, and in which He works. Blessed are those that walk with Him, and work with Him; they can tell of His mighty acts, and speak, of His wondrous works. Those that walk in this light, and are become children of this day, are witnesses of the true everlasting worship, which is *in the Spirit and in the Truth*. Such are come to the substance and end of all the legal administrations and temple worship, which consisted much in daily killing, and daily offering of bullocks, rams and lambs, and so on. Now those that are come to the worship in Spirit, *witness a daily dying, and a daily offering, till death is known*. Such know, that it is easier to kill a bullock or a ram outwardly, than to kill or mortify the beastly nature within: and it is a greater work to witness the will wholly resigned up into the will of the Lord, and the thoughts and imaginations brought down into the obedience of the cross, than to perform the outward part of worship, commanded in the law. I testify to all, that those who know not the beastly nature slain, and offered up in themselves, and their thoughts and will subjected, have not come to the end of the law, nor from under it, nor to the one everlasting offering, Christ Jesus.

V. It is very precious, not only when we meet together, but at all times, to *feel our minds exercised by, and meditating in, the law of the Lord*, which is spiritual. Those that are exercised in this law of the Spirit of Life, and walk in obedience to it, no evil nor temptation shall prevail against; but they will witness salvation for walls and bulwarks. Some were witnesses of old, that *the law of the Lord was pure and perfect*. Many are witnesses of the same this day, and know it so by the operation of it; and know themselves subjects of that law, which is spiritual within them, which judges every vain thought, and every idle word, and brings down every vain imagination. It is a blessed state, to be meditating in this law, day and night. For I testify, that this law of the Spirit of Life within, was man's rule, whereby he walked innocently and uprightly, before transgression entered, and before outward alphabets were invented, or before any outward law was written, or engraved on tables of stone. To this Spirit of Life within again are many called, and many are coming, and come to; and forever blessed are those that walk therein, and are ruled thereby.

Meditations & Experiences

VI. The *true knowledge of Jesus Christ* is very precious; to know Him as He was before *Abraham* was, and to know the knowledge of Him after the flesh passes away. Such know Him to be the tree of life, which grows in the midst of the garden of God, and they sit under His shadow with great delight, and His fruit is sweet to their taste. They that eat thereof know that food which the world is ignorant of, and is beyond words. Fruit and eating are more than words. Such are come to witness the gospel promises fulfilled, and they need no man to teach them; no man need to say to his neighbor, *know the Lord*; for the knowledge of Him abounds in their hearts.

That which makes the meetings of the righteous to differ from all other meetings in the world, is to feel Jesus, the Savior, in the midst of them, and to feel their hearts and minds in unity and fellowship with Him. This feeling and knowing, transcends all words and professions; for, for a time Christ's very disciples did not so know Him, while He was with them in that prepared body; therefore a remnant can call that day blessed, wherein their minds were turned from darkness within, to the Light within, which reveals and makes Christ manifest again, as He was with the Father before the world began, and as He was before *Abraham* was.

VII. It is now as truly witnessed as it was of old, *That the eye of the Lord runs to and fro through the earth, beholding the evil and the good*; specifically that eye which searches the heart, and tries the reins, and shows to man his thoughts. Our happiness consists in this, that we have a testimony within ourselves, that our hearts are upright and sincere in the sight of this eye. It is the upright heart which God has had respect for in all ages; for when his chosen people, the *Jews*, degenerated from uprightness of heart, notwithstanding they kept in the outward performances and observations, as keeping *appointed feasts, new moons, and sabbath-days, solemn assemblies, killing, and offering sacrifices*, and so on, yet all these things, while their hearts were gone astray from Him, and were not upright and sincere in the sight of this eye of the Lord, their performances were not accepted, but were an abomination unto Him.

It is a precious thing to witness, that our hearts are upright in the sight of the Lord, or before His eye, that runs to and fro through the earth; that that sin may never overtake us, which overtook the *Jews* of old, *namely to keep the outward form, and lose the power*. Our solemn assembling, our form of sound words, and our outward demeanor, which the Life of Truth led us into at first; if we feel not the same Life accompanying us, and preserving us in it, that we may be a living people, walking uprightly before the Lord; I say, without this, all is vain and unprofitable.

It is the honest and upright heart that is the good ground, where the seed of the kingdom grows and prospers, and brings forth acceptable fruit.

VIII. It is a very precious thing, to witness a *true waiting upon the Lord*. Many great and glorious promises are made to those that truly wait upon him. *They that wait upon the Lord shall lack no good thing*: this, to witness and enjoy, is the substance of all. While we waited upon invented means, men and books, upon our own thoughts and imaginations, our own wisdom and understanding, we lacked the good things; these were not sufficient to lead us to the knowledge, nor the enjoyment of them.

Hereby may all *Christendom*, so called, be tried and judged, specifically by this one word; they pretend a worshipping and waiting upon the Lord, but they lack the good things, and the evil things abound amongst them; so are hereby found false witnesses, those who say they wait upon the Lord, and that he has not fulfilled His promises to them. A remnant are at this day true and faithful witnesses, that the Lord is faithful, just and true to His promises, and that he has fitted and furnished them with the heavenly treasures, the good things of His kingdom, as they truly wait upon Him. This waiting does not begin when our solemn meetings begin, neither does it end with them, but remains always.

IX. The *Truth* in itself is very precious, and the revelation and knowledge of it in our hearts, is also very precious. It is in this *Truth*, that God is worshipped with that worship which is more acceptable than all the worships in the world whose worshippers profess the *Truth* in words, but know it not, neither are they made free by it; so are found false worshippers and false witnesses; for the revelation and knowledge of the *Truth* brings to freedom, freedom from sin; gives power over vain thoughts, over passions, over the will and inordinate affections, and also removes the ground from whence all evil springs.

The revelation and knowledge of this *Truth*, brings into that righteousness which exceeds the righteousness of the Scribes and Pharisees; it makes clean the inside. All other knowledge and religions in the world, makes clean but the outside, at most; but this the inside, and then the outside will be clean also.

Oh! what a lamentation may be taken up for the greater part of mankind, who are not only strangers to the revelation and powerful operation of the *Truth* in the inward parts, but also, through the wiles of the enemy of their soul's everlasting peace, are begotten into a belief, *That it is impossible to witness a clean inside, and to be delivered from all evil, on this side of the grave.* They are easily persuaded, that the enemy of their souls is always near them, ready on the right hand and on the left, to draw them aside into the way wherein they ought not to walk; but they have no knowledge nor faith in the heavenly *truth, virtue and power* present, which is able to save out of all temptations, and to deliver out of the snares of Satan; and therefore are taken captive at his pleasure.

In this state we ourselves were; but now the knowledge of the *Truth* is come, and the powerful operation of it we are witnesses of. Let us persevere and walk in the *Truth*, that we may witness the end of its work, which is to finish and make an end of sin, and bring in everlasting righteousness. This is the substance of all, and the end of the *Truth* revealing itself.

Now in the present sense and enjoyment of the revelation and knowledge of the powerful operation of the *Truth within*, in our own hearts, we cannot but call to mind the days past, in which the Lord waited to be gracious unto us, and followed us with His mercies and with His judgments; often knocking at the door of our hearts, and often appeared unto us, though we knew Him not; and His long-suffering was great, wherein He waited to show Himself kind and gracious unto us, standing at the door, until His locks were wet with the dew of the night, and we let Him not in, neither received His kindness, because we neither knew Him, nor His love.

But now He has revealed himself unto us, He has opened that spiritual eye in us that can see Him, and our hearts to receive Him, and has come to make His abode with us. Oh! Friends, how are we engaged to walk answerable to His great love, which we are made partakers of! Indeed *we love Him, because He first loved us.* We wait upon Him, because He first waited upon us. May not we say, as some of old said, *what manner of love is this, that we should be called the sons of God, and be inheritors of such precious promises*, and possessors of the knowledge of that one everlasting *Truth* which makes us free!

But friends, when the knowledge of this *Truth* is enjoyed, there is a possibility of losing it again; the Holy Spirit which seals and establishes in it, if it be grieved, it will not do its work; and *a vain thought, given place unto, will grieve* it; *an idle word will grieve it*; therefore it concerns us all, to wait and watch in that which preserves and keeps out of all evil, *that is to say*, the *Light*, for ever.

X. It is a blessed and happy state, to have *the testimony within ourselves*, that our minds are exercised in that wherein stands the everlasting universal worship, which is not limited to time or place.

This worship is not like the worships which are among the sects in the world, who pretend only to worship God in certain places, and at certain times, and think God is pleased with their pretended serving Him, one day in seven, or one hour in seven; though at other times they serve themselves, and the evil one, speak their own words, think their own thoughts, and do their own works.

OH! it is lamentable to behold, when I look over the state of *Christendom*, and see the apostasy it has degenerated into, retaining something of the form, but denying the Power.

Here is our blessedness and true happiness, that we have our minds exercised in the heavenly light that brings to, and preserves in the true everlasting worship which is inward, *in the Spirit and in the Truth;* which all *Temple* and *Jerusalem* worship, outwardly at certain times, and set places, were but a type and figure of. This worship *in the Spirit and in the Truth*, is the antitype, it is the substance of typical, temporary worships. Oh! my friends, let none of us be found out of this everlasting, universal worship, which does not begin when we meet together to wait upon the Lord a few hours, to be refreshed together in the sense of his presence; neither does it end when we part.

And friends, this rests upon my Spirit to testify, that none can enjoy true blessedness and spiritual consolation to their souls, farther than they have a testimony in themselves that they walk in the precious everlasting Light that now shines. To this Light in our minds we were at first turned, in which God dwells, and in which the worship *in Spirit and Truth* is learned and performed, in this age as in ages past. The way is, and has been, throughout all generations, ONE, and it is a plain pathway; the wayfaring man, though a fool, cannot err in it.

In this Light, many are now witnesses that God loved them, even while sinners; and that in the days of their darkness and ignorance, He waited upon them, to show Himself gracious; though then they had no faith in Him, no esteem for Him, neither could they see any comeliness in Him, *His visage being more marred than any man's*. Thus He appeared, until the Light shined out of the darkness, and gave the knowledge of His glory; which as they walked in, they became living witnesses of His power in salvation, redemption, and translation from darkness and the power of Satan, to the marvelous Light and Power of God; out of the corrupt nature and degradation, into the pure divine nature and regeneration; and so became plants and trees of righteousness, bearing fruit unto God, and giving Him the glory and praise of all His works, who alone is worthy throughout all generations, forever.

XI. It is a blessed state, *always to live in the sense and feeling of that love which first visited us, wherein* our minds were turned to the Light, which shined in the darkness; for we were then darkness; which Light then made manifest and revealed to us the *gift of God* given to us, which is compared to a little leaven, to a grain of seed, to a pearl hid in the field. It is precious to know the *leaven to work*, the *seed to grow*, the *field to be purchased*, and the *pearl found; bought and possessed*. This is more than talk and profession.

Now can many say, as was witnessed of old, *we are come unto Him as unto a living stone, elect and precious, and we are kept by the power of Him unto salvation, and we are in Him in whom there is no condemnation:* Thus to read and witness the scriptures, is beyond all the talk and notions that are in the world, which lays in wickedness, where the guilt and condemnation is.

As we continually live in the sense and feeling of that precious love which at first sought us out, and pulled some of us as brands out of the fire, and others as swine wallowing in the mire; as we remain sensible of this love, we shall feel our hearts more and more engaged to walk worthy of it; *and not only profess grace, but live under it; not only profess the Light, but walk in it, that we may be perfect children of it;* for if we live not the life of what we profess, harsher judgments will pursue us than many others who are called as we are, but have not tasted of the heavenly Power as we have. Therefore it concerns, us to be watchful, and retain our first love; for it is possible, after the house *is swept and garnished, and the unclean spirits cast forth, that they may return and enter again.* Therefore it is very precious, not only to know that blessed Power that castes forth the unclean spirit, and sweeps and garnishes the house with heavenly treasures; but also to dwell and abide in the same, by it to be preserved from being defiled again. This is the substance of the *Christian Religion*. This is the end of all ministering, speaking and writing. This is more than hearing ten thousand sermons. Let us always remain in the feeling of, and obedience to this Power, and we shall never fall.

XII. It is more than words can express, *to feel and enjoy that wherein the kingdom of heaven stands*. It is written in the Holy Scriptures, *that the kingdom of heaven stands not in food and drinks, and outward washings; but in the Power and joy of the Holy Spirit*. To enjoy this, is the substance of all; but none come to receive the joy of the Holy Spirit, but such only who are kept by the Power in which the kingdom stands; which Power preserves from evil, and keeps from falling into temptation. Many may come to the knowledge of this Power, and may possess it and have some faith in it; which is beyond all notional sectarians in Christendom; yet if they live not obedient to it, and witness a being kept by it to the end, they come not to be children of this kingdom, nor to sit down in it, nor enjoy the comfort and pleasures thereof.

The bare profession and knowledge of the Power is of little worth, but a being preserved by it; for if any enter into evil and temptation, such grieve the Holy Spirit, so cannot have the joy of it, wherein the kingdom stands. This is that which chiefly distinguishes us from the diverse sects in *Christendom*, a being *preserved in the Power*, and not a *talking of it only*. It is written in the Holy Scriptures of Truth, that Christ Jesus the second *Adam*, when He was tempted by the devil with harsh and grievous temptations, *ate nothing*, but by the Power of his father that dwelt in him, withstood the devil and all his temptations; and when he departed from Him, *angels ministered unto Him*. This same Power which preserves in temptations, and keeps from eating or receiving the bait of the enemy or tempter, are we all to witness in the time of trial, and hour of temptation.

It was the first *Adam* that ate when he was tempted; now his eating implied a taking or letting in something, a giving place to the devil's bait, whereby the temptation entered. He did not stand in the Power wherein the heavenly kingdom stands, which is able to preserve, as did the second *Adam*: so departing from this, he lost the joy of the Holy Spirit, which the kingdom stands in; as all the children of the first *Adam* do, who have not faith in that Power that saves out of temptation.

This is the substance of the *Christian Religion*, which we are called to the profession and possession of, namely, *the Power and joy of the Holy Spirit, in which the kingdom stands;* which Power strikes at the root of all the wickedness and evil in the world, and is the axe that is laid to the root of the evil tree, which has grown up in the apostasy. This is that by which *Christendom* must be reformed. There is no sound reformation but by this, *the Power and joy of the Holy Spirit,* both in the individual, and in the people in general.

Friends are witnesses, and many could seal it with their lives, that there is no other way nor means appointed of God, to come to sit down in the kingdom of heaven, nor to attain everlasting salvation, but by believing in the Power of God, in the Light of Christ *within,* to which our minds have been directed. Indeed, among the many sects in *Christendom,* there are diverse other means and ways invented and set up; but we know them all to be vanity. We have tried and proved them, and know there is nothing of worth in them. We are now come to the true and living way, the ancient path, in which the righteous in all ages ever walked. Now this remains, that we always feel our hearts engaged to walk in this way, and to keep sensible of that Power which saves from evil, that we may adorn our profession; for if any, that profess this everlasting way, enter into temptation, or commit evil, they do not adorn their profession, but are a scandal to it, and lay a stumbling-block in the way of others, who are where we were, when wandering in desolate places, and traveling in the desert howling wilderness. The day of such will be turned into darkness, and the curse due to him that lays a stumbling-block in the way of the blind, and that leads him out of his way, will fall upon them.

Therefore it concerns all to be watchful, and persevere in that which is good, to be as lights of the world, and as the salt of the earth indeed; that we may never leave shining, nor lose our Savior. Whatsoever was written before, was written for our education; and it is profitable to meditate and consider, that many in former ages had much experience of the Power and presence of the Lord, saw many of his wondrous works, and traveled through the Red Sea and Wilderness, to the borders of the promised land; yet through murmuring and disobedience entered not therein, nor did enjoy the end of the Lord, in bringing them out of *Egypt's* land. And many may in this age fall short, as those before did, if we walk not close with the Lord, and learn, by what is written, to take warning, lest by disobedience and unbelief, we fall short of receiving the great recompense of reward.

XIII. The *bread of the kingdom* is the joy of the Holy Spirit, felt and known *within,* which satisfies and refreshes the soul. This bread is the spiritual nourishment, which comes down from heaven. The shewbread, in the outward temple, was a type and figure of this bread, which is indeed the antitype and substance thereof. The table, in the outward temple of the Lord, was furnished with outward bread: As we witness our bodies to be the temple of the Lord, we shall enjoy this spiritual nourishment which the shewbread that was in the outward temple was but the type and shadow of. This is the nourishment that fills and satisfies the spiritually hungry, when husks and all outside things cannot.

XIV. Many are living witnesses in this day, as of old, *that the foundation of God stands sure*; and that this foundation, as now made manifest, was the foundation of the righteous in all ages; that the Light, grace and Spirit of God within, which mixes not with vain thoughts and evil imaginations, but discovers them and judges them, is this foundation. This is the stone the builders in their natural wisdom reject and despise, and cry up other stones, and invent other foundations, according to the imaginations of their own hearts.

Now it is a blessed thing, and the duty of every single individual, to witness themselves as living stones, built upon this foundation, and to have their hearts and minds united to it, and framed with it.

XV. The same grace, the same anointing, *which was the saints' teacher in the primitive times*, is revealed and witnessed in this our day and time. It is a blessed thing always to learn from Him; for many that have come to the revelation of this teacher, not waiting low in that which did reveal Him, that the self might be made of no importance, and the will and selfish spirit brought down. They have been deceived, and have learned from the false teacher, the antichrist, instead of the true, living Christ. Yet under the name of the true; this has happened in some among ourselves, since we were a people; understand this, that no people ever worshipped the whore, the mother of harlots, the beast, false prophet and antichrist, under those names and denominations; but being deceived, gave them good names and believed her to be the true woman, the Lamb's wife, the true prophet, and the true Christ. This has been the state of all the apostates in *Christendom*; for as the mystery of godliness is great, so is the mystery of iniquity great also; and there is none but those that come truly to learn of the grace of God, the anointing within, that are able to discern between the true and the false.

Meditations & Experiences

Therefore it is precious always to learn of the grace and anointing, and to walk in the Light which our minds were at first directed to; this reveals the deep things of God, and finds out the hidden things of *Esau*.

The very remembrance of the time wherein our minds were turned from the ways, inventions and teachings of men *without*, to the Light, grace and anointing *within*, is very precious; for hereby we are made partakers of a measure of the same wisdom and revelation, which *John* wrote about in his book of the Revelation.

The same Spirit, which *John* was led by, to give names to things according to their nature, and not according to appearance, is now again witnessed. The great whore, the mother of harlots, the beast and false prophet, and the golden cup that is held forth to the nations, the antichrist in the temple, and the great red dragon that *John* saw in heaven, by the same Spirit are now revealed and judged; and as we keep our hearts and ears open to this teacher, we can never be deceived by them again.

All the nominal professors and sects in *Christendom*, who learn not from this teacher, are so completely deceived, that they believe the whore is the Lamb's wife, and her golden cup, the cup of blessing; and so are greedily drinking of it; not discerning the false prophet and antichrist from the true, because he gets into the temple of God, and clothes himself as if an angel of light, and as if the true Christ; such take the great red dragon, that appears in heaven, to be the Lamb of God.

Therefore it is a blessed thing, always to keep our minds stayed, and our feet walking in the heavenly light that now shines, which reveals the true teacher, that teaches and discovers all things, and gives to see to the ground and foundation of things; to discern spirits; and keep out of that wherein the mystery of iniquity prevails.

All the teachings of men and books in the world are but dross and dung in comparison of this divine teacher, the *Light, Spirit,* and *Grace of God within.* This was man's teacher and guide before books were written; before an outward law was written; and this I testify, in the word of the Lord, that teachings of all men, books and writings, which tend to divert the mind of mankind from this divine teacher within, are vain and unprofitable, and proceed from that wisdom which is earthly, sensual and devilish; and all that lend an ear to it, are captivated in the mystery of iniquity: ever learning, and never able to come to the knowledge of the Truth which makes free, so long as they abide under such teachers.

Many are living witnesses, that as they surrendered themselves to be taught, and led by the true teacher, the anointing within, they soon became wiser than all their former teachers.

XVI. The same everlasting Power, which preserved the righteous in all ages past out of evil, and from falling into temptations, is now *revealed and witnessed in this our day and age*; specifically the same Power and arm of salvation that preserved *Joseph* in *Egypt*, *Job* in all his trials and temptations, *Daniel* and the three children, and all the primitive prophets and *Christians*, out of all the fiery trials, assaults and buffetings of Satan, they were met with.

Therefore it is a blessed thing to be truly acquainted with this Power, and always to live in the sense of it; for it is possible that people may come to the knowledge of this Power, and make a profession of it, and witness salvation and redemption by it, in a great measure; yet if they wait not low in their minds, till it has fully wrought the work of salvation and redemption in them, or wholly brought every thought and imagination into the obedience of Christ, subdued their own wills and selfish spirits, and know their self made of no importance and nailed to the cross; I say, without this, they may fall into the snare of the devil again, be captivated and led into temptation again; for it is about such, the tempter and destroyer goes like a roaring lion seeking to devour, specifically those, out of whom he has been cast and dispossessed. It is written, *He rules in the Hearts of the Children of disobedience.* He needs not go about such, being got within them; there he is in his throne.

But it is about the righteous, out of whom he has been cast, *he goes*, who are redeemed from under his Power, and translated out of his kingdom; it is against such he appears, not only like a roaring lion, but as a subtle serpent, and angel of light.

Therefore it is a blessed thing, always to live in the sense, knowledge and feeling of this ancient Power, which alone saves and delivers in the midst of all trials and besetments of the evil one; as the eye of the mind and understanding is fixed upon it, no temptation can prevail; and to know your Faith increased in it; for faith in this Power of God is compared to a shield, which is able to quench all the fiery darts of the devil, and to give victory over him. Now that which was our misery and loss in the time of our ignorance and darkness, is the misery and loss of mankind in their unregenerate state. We had no faith in the Spirit of God, which convinced the world of sin. We did not believe, that the same hand of Power that smote us for sin and transgression, was able and sufficient to heal us; neither did we regard the strivings of God's Spirit within; neither did we give heed to Him that stood at the door of our hearts and knocked, who long waited to show Himself gracious unto us; and was as a light shining in darkness, but we regarded it not, and so did not know the virtue and powerful operation of it. In this unbelieving, disobedient state, we were children of wrath as well as others, but having obtained mercy to be faithful, we have now, with the Power from our faith in the Spirit of God, left all the world that is captivated, by reason of their unbelief and hardness of heart.

And herein is the love, exceeding kindness and mercy of God manifest, in that He loved us, while we were enemies; and waited to show Himself gracious, while we were sinners; to be reconciled unto us, when we were in rebellion against Him; and enlightened us, when we were darkness; and often called, when we were running from Him; and was near and ready to teach us, when we were ignorant and did not desire the knowledge of His ways. In this was the exceeding love of God manifest to us then, and is the same to all the world now. His love is universal to all, as is testified in the holy scriptures; *God so loved the world, that He gave his only begotten Son a light into the World; that whosoever believeth in him should not perish, but have everlasting Life.*

It is very precious to walk in this light, which does reveal the love and kindness of God, and brings to the knowledge and experience of the means of salvation which He has appointed; and to the feeling of that Power, which saves from falling into temptation, specifically the same Power, which preserved Jesus when He was tempted in the wilderness. Now if any, that are come to the knowledge and profession of this Power, are not preserved by it from falling into temptation, and delivered from evil, such are not obedient nor faithful to it, so do not adorn their profession; *such do not glorify the Power, but are as spots in our feasts, and a scandal to the Gospel of Peace, and enemies to the Cross of Christ, which is the Power of God to Salvation.*

Now those that live in, and are obedient to this Power are the wisest, happiest, and safest people in the world; blessed above all the families of the earth, blessed with an hundred fold in this world, and in the world to come life everlasting. Such are the salt of the earth which seasons all things, as a city on a hill, which cannot be hid, and as the light of the world indeed.

XVII. Many are living witnesses, that *the law of the Spirit of Life*, unto which their minds have been directed, *is pure and perfect*. They witness it so by its operation in them, by which every appearance of evil is condemned.

It is the happiness of every individual, to have the witness or testimony within them, that they love this law, and that they meditate in it day and night. *Oh!* said one of old, *how I love your law!* It is only those that love it, that are true witnesses of its purity and perfection, for it is possible, that a person or people may not only profess and talk of this law, but come to some knowledge of it also, and yet not love it, nor meditate in it, nor feel the power and peace of it.

Those that love the law of God, are converted, and made wise unto salvation by it; and though their enemies are very many, and very near also, yet they cannot prevail against them that love this law. They are the happiest people of all the families of the earth. No evil prevails against such; and as has been witnessed of old, *namely, Great peace has those that love your law*. So those are living witnesses of the same *great peace* in this age, who loves the law, which is Light. *Your law is light*, said one. He that loves the Light, brings his deeds unto it, by it to be tried and judged; and after this, the *great peace* is witnessed. Peace is the reward of those that love the law of God; peace in the inward, spiritual parts, specifically the Peace of God, which the world cannot give nor take away.

This one word or sentence may try all the sects in *Christendom*, and others who profess themselves lovers of the law of God, yet have not peace in their dwellings; these have not the answer of a good conscience, which keeps void of offence towards God and man. They have not that peace which passes the understanding of man in the fall; they know not their hearts and minds kept by it; but are found in the evil-doing, where the tribulation and anguish is, and in that fear which brings torment. *So where the doing of evil is, the law is not loved.* Let your talk and profession be what it will, what is written is infallibly true: *He that does evil hates the light*; and he that hates the Light is wicked, to whom there is no peace; the law being no Light to his feet, nor lantern to his path. He walks in darkness and stumbles, and knows not at what; and in the end, lies down in sorrow.

Therefore it is very good for every individual, not only to know the law of God, but also to live in the sense and love of this law at all times; when they are about their common occasions in the world, as well as in their solemn assembling before the Lord. The love of this pure law of the Spirit of Life, which judges every appearance of evil, makes one wise unto salvation, wiser than all former teachers; and to hear, love and obey this law, or word in the heart, is the end of all words, outward dispensations and ministrations, though proceeding from the Power of God itself. For had not mankind, degenerated from the love and obedience of this law, or command of God, then transgression would have never entered, neither would sin have a being in the heart of man, nor would an outward law have been added or given forth. *The outward law was added because of transgressions, and has power over the transgressor, so long as he lives disobedient, and a stranger to the inward law, written in the table of the heart by the finger of God.* The inward law existed before an outward law was written, either in a book or on tables of stone, and before the cause of it was brought forth into the world.

XVIII. The *day-spring* from on high, and the *everlasting Light* has and does shine out of darkness in the hearts of many in this age; and they are, by the heavenly shining thereof, come to the knowledge of the field where the treasure is hid, and to the sight of that, whose worth and beauty transcends all the treasures and pleasures this world can afford. None are to rest in the bare knowledge of the field, but to sell all and purchase it.

All the sects in *Christendom*, who believe not in the Light within, and despise the day of its appearance within themselves, are so far from enjoying this heavenly treasure that they are wholly ignorant of the place or field wherein it is hid.

This knowledge is sealed in the hearts of a remnant, that there is no other way, no other means, no other key to be found to open the heavenly mysteries, nor to unloose the seals thereof, and to lead into the enjoyment of the heavenly treasure, but the holy divine Light, which in their hearts has appeared and shined gloriously, to the discovery and destruction of the man of sin and mystery of iniquity, which once wrought and ruled therein. In this light they have believed and walked, and seen the wondrous works of the Lord in the deep, while the people and nations, that despise and hate it, walk and dwell in darkness, and in the region and shadow of death, where the spiritual poverty, woe and misery is; where the stumbling, groping, falling, and wandering in desolate places is; where the laboring for vanity, and lying down in sorrow is; therefore are the hearts of such greatly engaged unto the Lord, to walk worthy of the riches of his grace, light and heavenly treasure, he has made them partakers of.

XIX. The light of the glorious gospel *now shines*; the day of salvation *has come*, specifically the salvation from God, which he has prepared before the face of all people.

This is the day of great salvation, which many righteous men and prophets saw afar off, and prophesied of, that is now revealed to us. It is a blessed thing, not only to know the appearance of the day of salvation, but to know the joy of it, the joy of God's salvation; and to know it as a fortification, to save and defend, not only from the besieger without, but from the enemy within also.

This is the glorious Light of the Gospel, that shines in this day of salvation now revealed, which as we walk and abide in, we shall be as strong as an army with banners, and witness victory over our enemies within, which are our greatest enemies. To be saved from the deception of thinking our own thoughts, and speaking our own words, and doing our own works that are not divinely inspired. This is the great salvation that brings us to the sabbath of rest; to the keeping of the holy-day to the Lord. One that enjoyed this salvation, asked this question; *how can we escape, if we neglect so great salvation?* It is a question that includes an impossibility; for there is no escaping the wrath to come, by those that neglect this great salvation that has now appeared unto them, there being no other way nor means appointed of God besides this gospel Light, or great day of salvation, which to us has appeared.

This is my testimony, that none can receive the joy of God's salvation, enter into the sabbath of rest, or keep holy-day to the Lord, further than they know a ceasing, and a being saved from thinking their own vain thoughts, following their own wills, and obeying their own wisdom; for the selfish thoughts that arise within, are the root of evil, and as the foundation of the kingdom of darkness; and the light of this day of salvation, is as the axe laid to the root of the evil tree.

So it is a blessed thing for people to meet and wait together, and walk in this heavenly light and day of salvation, which discovers and judges every vain thought and foolish imagination, subdues them, and brings them down into the obedience of Christ. In this, as they walk and abide, they truly differ from all other families of the earth; for in this heavenly *gospel Light*, which judges every appearance of evil, stands the true fellowship and true unity. It is the foundation of that Church, against which the gates of hell shall never prevail; as they walk and dwell therein, the power of death and hell shall never break them, but they shall remain as Mount Zion, which can never be removed. In this stands their happiness and safety: Out of this, they are as weak as other people.

XX. It is a blessed thing, to wait for the *appearance of Him* who is the consolation of *Israel*, and for *the coming of His kingdom*; but it is more blessed to be witnesses of His appearance, and to know His kingdom come; and most blessed of all, to know a sitting down in it with Him, in the glory of His Father, and our Father, His God, and our God.

XXI. It is a blessed thing, truly to *know how to wait for the appearance of Jesus*, and to know Him *when He does appear*; I say, this is very blessed; but it is more blessed, or a greater degree of blessedness, to be witnesses of His appearance, and to join with Him when He does appear; and so to experience the end of His appearance accomplished, abiding with Him till it be finished; truly understanding the end wherefore He does appear, and their state and condition at His appearance. This is the main thing chiefly to be understood, and minded throughout all dispensations.

And under them all, he is to be carefully minded and regarded, though it be in his first or lowest appearance, which is to convince of sin, self-righteousness and judgment; in order to destroy sin; finish transgression, and bring in everlasting righteousness. Unless people abide with him, and love his appearance in the ministration of condemnation, which brings tribulation and anguish upon the soul that has sinned, they can never come to enjoy and inherit the ministration of life and salvation, nor never come to enjoy the glory of his appearance the second time, without sin unto salvation.

This is the loss and misery of mankind, and was our loss and misery in the day of our ignorance, that we knew not how to wait for the appearance of Christ, or the coming of the just one; neither do they, nor did we, know him when he did appear; for he often appeared unto us, and stood at the door of our hearts, and knocked, and waited to show himself gracious unto us; but we not knowing it was he, did not regard him, nor open unto him; yet he was indeed the desire of our hearts, and he whom we longed to enjoy, and is the desire of all nations, the light and salvation of the *Gentiles*, the consolation and glory of *Israel*; but in this was our loss and misery, that we knew not how to wait for his appearance, neither did we know him when he did appear. So I say again, it is a blessed thing, for a people to know how to wait for the appearance of Jesus, the Savior, and to know him when he does appear.

But behold, this is a greater degree of blessedness, to be witnesses of his appearance, and to know the *coming of the just One*, or *the rising of the Sun of Righteousness, with healing under his wings*, and to be able to say, with the primitive *Christians, We know that the Son of God is come, and has given us an understanding, whereby we know him that is true, and are in him that is true, specifically in his Son Jesus Christ; this is the true God and eternal Life*. This is a high and heavenly knowledge, and a blessed state. This is the mark and prize of the high calling of God in Christ Jesus, we have been called unto; and this is the state all are to wait for, inherit and possess, and not to sit down short of it. If this be not witnessed and enjoyed, all profession is vain, all knowledge is vain, all Religion and talk of *Christianity* is vain, and of no worth; for it is he that believes that Christ is come *in the flesh*, and that demonstrates the livingness of his Faith by the works thereof, that is *of God*, and *God dwells in him*, and *he in God*. This is more than a bare profession, or verbal confession, according to the testimony of *John*, the Divine, in his first Epistle, chapter IV.

XXII. It was a spiritual and heavenly Vision which the Prophet *Daniel* had, when he saw the interpretation of the king's dream; *a stone cut out of the mountain without hands, smite at the feet of the image, and break in pieces the Iron, the Brass, the Clay, the Silver, the Gold, and become a great Mountain that filled the whole Earth*. A remnant in this age are come to the same everlasting Light and spiritual Eye, whereby they see the Power of God, signified by that stone, prevail against all *imagery*, not only without, but within also; and know the ground of it shaken and removed. The dark thoughts and imaginations of men, are the grounds of the imagery upon the face of the earth; and that Power that breaks them down, and brings every thought into the obedience of Christ, is the antitype of that stone, and its work revealed to *Daniel*, and dreamed of by the king. In this day of light and knowledge some are come to witness this little stone become a great mountain, and to fill the Earth, and to be the chief foundation, and corner stone, elect and precious; the rock and hiding place of the righteous in this, and all ages. These abide in it, whereby they are preserved from making likenesses and images to themselves, either of things in Heaven, or things on earth; and out of the many mixtures prefigured by the iron, brass, clay, silver, gold, and the defiling and corrupting themselves therewith. There is not another means of preservation, nor of coming to receive the white stone, which *John*, in his vision and **revelation** saw, wherein is the new name written, which none knows save he that **has it. This** is the name, which is better than the name of sons or daughters. *He that reads let him understand, and give God the glory forever.*

XXIII. This I testify, that the way of life and **everl**asting happiness, the way that brings to the sitting down in the kingdom of God, with *Abraham, Isaac and Jacob*, which was the way of the righteous in all ages, *is now again revealed and made known*. This way is the true everlasting light that now shines, not only in darkness, but out of it; which light is the thing our minds were at first turned to, which judges every appearance of evil, every vain thought and evil motion that arises within; and as there is a walking in this way, a sitting down in the kingdom will be experienced; for we have been and are called to inherit substance, to possess life, and to sit down with Christ in heavenly places.

So it is a precious thing, for all that know this way, to persevere in it till they possess these things, and in the same abide; which way is the light of Christ within, and there is not another; and the walking in this way distinguishes them from all the nominal professors upon the face of the earth, specifically this light that judges every appearance of evil.

It is a precious state, to feel the mind stayed upon the Lord, walking in his way; to know the girdle and bridle of *Truth*, and a being girded and bridled with it; to know every high thought and imagination, brought down and subjected unto Christ *the light, the way.* This is possible to be known now, as in time past. It is in the thoughts, will and imaginations, that the enemy of man's happiness gets and builds his strong holds; and until they are broken down, subjected and destroyed by the Power of God within, no peace, quietness, and soul satisfaction, can be enjoyed; no sitting down in the kingdom of God, nor drinking of the rivers of pleasure that are at his right hand, can be attained to or partaken of.

XXIV. It is as truly witnessed now, as in days of old, that to be *spiritually-minded is life and peace*; to mind the Spirit, to have our minds, thoughts and wills exercised by the Spirit of truth, is *life and peace;* and to be carnally-minded is *death, sorrow and trouble.* These things are not only read, but truly known, and every individual may feel both within.

XXV. It is as we meet, and wait together, *in the Spirit*, as we live and walk *in the Spirit*, the worship of God in Spirit and truth is performed; which all the bare professors upon the face of the earth are ignorant of. Such as wait and worship in the Spirit, know Jesus in the midst of them to be their Savior, teacher and leader; and as they follow and obey him, though but as one of a family, and two of a tribe, they will be as the light of the world, as the salt of the earth, and patterns and examples of righteousness to all that behold them.

XXVI. It is a precious thing, for every individual *to know the right arm of the Lord, which brings salvation*, and to *witness a sitting down at his right hand*, where the sheep stand, where the rivers of pleasures run softly, and to drink of the same, which refresh the whole city of God. To feel this arm of the Lord, and to know it revealed, and to come to a sitting down at his right hand, is the end, sum and substance of the *Christian* religion; such know salvation for walls and bulwarks, and are as Mount Zion, which cannot be moved.

XXVII. It is a very blessed state, always to live, walk, meet together, and wait in that which *gives free access* to the throne of grace, and which leads into the presence of Him that sits thereon; in whose presence, some of old could witness, *were rivers of pleasures, and at his right hand, joy for evermore*. Oh! all that taste of one drop of this river, and partake of the least measure of this joy, know them to over-balance and outweigh all the treasures, joys and pleasure, this world and the glory of it can afford.

XXVIII. The light, to which our minds have been turned, was the *watch-tower* of the righteous in all ages, and is the same to the righteous in this age; and all people upon the face of the earth, and all pretended watchmen in *Christendom*, who watch not in this tower, *watch in vain; and see nothing that profits*. This is the word of truth to all *Christendom*, and all people.

This light is the one everlasting way that leads unto him that fits and prepares to enter the kingdom of heaven, gives free access to God, and the throne of his grace, and presents unto him without spot or wrinkle. Many are witnesses of the beginning of this blessed work, and have received that faith, whereby they believe the accomplishment of it; in which, as they live and abide, the blessed experience of the finishing of it shall be added to their faith.

XXIX. It is a good state, for every individual *to wait in silence upon the Lord;* such only come to witness obedience to those divine precepts left upon record in the holy scriptures, *be still, and know that I am God; let all flesh be silent before* *the Lord*. Thus to wait and to worship in the heavenly Spirit that brings to *stillness*; to a *standing still and beholding the salvation of God; to* the *silence of all flesh within;* to the *stopping all voices and motions to evil within,* and to the *obeying of the voice and Power of God within*: This is the worship of God in the Spirit and in the truth, in the inward parts, which God loves, specifically to worship and obey, and follow the appearance and manifestation of the Spirit of God within. This worship, the world and the high professors in it are strangers to. In this we differ from them all, specifically as we are found waiting and worshipping in that which silences all flesh, and brings to the standing still, and beholding the salvation of God.

The Spirit of truth, which convinces the world of sin, is that wherein the universal worship of God stands, and is performed. This I testify of it, that there is power and sufficiency in it, not only to convince of sin, reprove and condemn for sin, but also to convert, change, cleanse, and redeem the whole world of mankind from sin, if they would believe in it, love it, receive it and obey it. *This is the condemnation of the world, that light is come into it, and they love darkness rather*, and will not bring their deeds to the light, love, believe nor walk in it; so that saying of Christ is verified upon them, *unless you believe that I am he, you shall die in your sins, and whither I go, you cannot come.*

Many are witnesses of the power and sufficiency of this Spirit of Truth, and of its redeeming power from sin, and to the strength of it: so are not convinced by it as the world is, being redeemed from committing of it; they know it to be their comforter and leader into all truth. It is very precious to be found in the true disciples' state, waiting for the comfort and leading of the Spirit of truth, and witnessing the same within themselves. A remnant in this day, who have received this Spirit, and followed the leadings of it, are able to say as some of old did, *we are not come to Mount Sinai, where the voice of words is heard, where the thundering, lightning, and earthquakes are, but to Mount Zion, the city of the living God, the heavenly Jerusalem;* and to *an innumerable company of angels;* to the *general assembly and church of the first-born, which are written in heaven,* and to *God the judge of all;* to the *spirits of just men made perfect;* to *Jesus, the mediator of the new covenant,* and *to the blood of sprinkling, that speaks better things than that of* Abel. This is a high and heavenly state, which the primitive *Christians* were come unto, while in their earthly tabernacles they enjoyed the heavenly treasure. Such have the witness in themselves, that they are inhabitants and fellow citizens of this heavenly *Jerusalem*, whereunto no unclean thing can enter; specifically while they dwell in these houses of clay; they walk in this city, and have their conversation in heaven with God, Christ, and holy or just men's spirits made perfect. This the spirit of this world, though clothed with the name of Christianity, cannot bear.

XXX. It is a very blessed state, to be found true waiters for, and witnesses of *the second coming of Christ, which is without sin unto salvation*; for true happiness does not consist in having seen one of the days of the son of man; or in being witnesses of his first appearance, wherein he convinces and reproves for sin; but in waiting for the witnessing his second coming to cleanse, save and redeem from sin: herein is the joy of God's salvation felt and enjoyed.

Christ's appearance is first to convince of sin; and this is a ministration of condemnation, which is glorious in its time; but there is a ministration which exceeds in glory, which all are to wait for witness, and not sit down short of. This is the mark of the high calling, the high and heavenly state which they are called to, specifically to know the second coming of Christ without sin unto salvation, and a being presented to the father without spot or wrinkle. This to possess and enjoy, is the end, sum and substance of all the dispensations of God towards mankind ever since the fall. This is the end of all good words and writings, and the end of Christ's first and second appearance.

All men have sinned and come short of the glory of God, therefore must know the ministration of judgment, and condemnation fulfilled in and upon them, before they can know the glory that is in it, and before they come to know the second ministration, which exceeds in glory.

It is a precious thing to be *inward with the Lord*, and to feel our hearts drawn near unto him, waiting for the appearance of Christ, that when he does appear, we may appear with him in glory. This is the high and heavenly state that some were in, when they could say, *truly our fellowship is with the Father and with the Son*. This to witness, is the feast of fat things prophesied of, and the broad rivers and streams, which make glad the city of God, beyond what all the delicacies of the earth can afford. This is the soul's delight, rest, and happiness, which some did enjoy in former ages, as a remnant do in this age, praises to God forever.

To mind the Spirit, or to be spiritually-minded, not only in our solemn meetings, but at all times is our duty, and very precious: Then will the testimony of one in the primitive times be found true, when he said to be *spiritually-minded is life and peace*, death and trouble are taken away, the ministration of condemnation is ended, having done its work; the word which was as a hammer, fire and sword, has broken down, burnt up, destroyed and purged away the filth of the daughter of *Jerusalem*, and is now become as milk, honey and balm: and as a glorious light that shines more and more unto the perfect day; as a shield, fortress and tower of defense, where everlasting peace and safety is; salvation being as walls and bulwarks, against which the enemy cannot prevail, nor nothing that would defile enter. In this state some were in the primitive times, when they could say, *we can do nothing against the Truth, but for it*; and it is possible to say and do the same now.

XXXI. It is a blessed thing for a man to know within himself, and from a living experience to be able to say, as one of old did, *the Lord is my Shepherd, I shall not lack*. Such are witnesses of the truth of those sayings of Christ Jesus, *my sheep hear my voice, and I know them, and they follow me, and I give unto them eternal life; and they shall never perish, neither shall any man pluck them out of my Father's Hand*. It is as this voice is heard, obeyed and followed; that a leading out of that state, where the wants are, is witnessed, into the green pastures, where the true and safe feeding is; where the lying down in the valley is; where none can make afraid; where the Bread is sure and the Water fails not: And this I testify, all that do not hear and obey this heavenly voice of the true Shepherd, are goats and swine, and not Sheep; let them profess what they will, they feed upon husks, and are wandering in the dry places, and upon the barren Mountains where the wants are, and the green pastures of Life and Salvation they are strangers to.

XXXII. It is a very blessed thing for people to know *how to worship God aright*, and to be *found in this worship*, not only at set times and appointed places, but at all times, and in all places. This is the spiritual worship, or the worship in Spirit and in truth; and these are the spiritual worshippers, which God seeks and accepts. This worship excels all other worships upon the face of the earth at set times and appointed places, which stand in saying so many prayers in a day, and reading and singing so many lessons a day, and hearing so many sermons a day, and other outward observations. This worship stands in time, place, letter and form; but they that worship God aright; it is in the Spirit and in the truth, which is pure and universal.

Meditations & Experiences

As people are found in this worship, they differ from and excel all others upon the face of the earth. These worshippers know what it is to bow at the name of Jesus; what it is to know every thought brought into the obedience of Christ; what his Rule, Government, and great Authority is; and how all power in Heaven and Earth is given unto him; and how all are to worship him as they worship the Father, whether things in Heaven, or things on Earth, or things under the Earth. These can confess with their tongues that Jesus Christ is Lord, to the glory of God the Father, truly and experimentally being witnesses of his heavenly power and rule in their hearts, minds, and understandings, giving victory over all vain thoughts, self-will, carnal desires, and wanderings of the mind. These are the worshippers that know the old man put off with his deeds, and the new man put on; the old things cast away, and all things become new; and what it is to enjoy the sabbath of rest, where the end is put to the thinking of their own thoughts, and speaking their own words, and doing their own works; and what it is to bear no burden upon the Sabbath-day; and what it is to enjoy the comfort of the Scriptures, and to enjoy the good things they testify of. What the righteous in all ages did enjoy such are partakers of, and are in unity with just men's spirits, being come to God, the judge of all, who is blessed forever.

Our peace, joy, consolation, and continual happiness stand in this, in being exercised in this worship, witnessing the Power of God, the name of Jesus, over all in ourselves, all bowing under it, and yielding obedience thereto, as in innocence before transgression, *where the Earth was subdued in the dominion of God, and the heavenly rule was over all.* This, the true worship, in the Spirit, and in the truth, brings again into, and makes free from the contrary, as truly as testified in the Scriptures: *If you know the Truth, the Truth shall make you free:* free from the evil that is in the world, from the evils within, and from the enemies within, which are the greatest enemies. Unless this freedom be known, all other knowledge is vain; all religion and profession vain; all talk of God, Christ, and *Christianity*, vain.

XXXIII. Blessed are those who have their minds and hearts always exercised by that which *leads into the fellowship of just men's spirits made perfect.* Such have also, unity with their words and testimonies, left upon record in the Scriptures of Truth, as is written by one in the Psalms, *Blessed is the man that walks not in the counsel of the ungodly, nor stands in the way of sinners; nor sits in the seat of the scornful; but his delight is in the Law of the Lord, and*

Meditations & Experiences

therein does he meditate day and night. The same blessed state is to be witnessed now, which is more than to read and sing all the Psalms; and he is the only blessed man that does those things. If *Christendom* had learned this lesson, which they have read and sung, they would not have become as a waste howling wilderness, and as a desert which brings forth no fruit to God, having lent their ear to the wicked one, and walked in the way of sinners so long, till they are brought to believe, that it is impossible to walk in any other way, while on this side the grave.

In this condition we ourselves were, while the veil of the covering was over our hearts. We dwelt in this thick darkness, where the lending the ear to the wicked is, where the way of the sinner and seat of the scornful is, and knew not the way out of it. That which dispersed this thick darkness, took away the veil from off our heart, stopped the ear that hearkened to the wicked one, blinded that eye which led to walk in the way of sinners, and brought down that exalted spirit that sat in the seat of the scornful; I say, that which has done this for us, was, and is no other than the Power of God working in his precious Light, to which our minds were at first turned, and in which we have believed; which, as we walk and abide in, we witness such sayings as these in Scripture fulfilled, *They that see shall be made blind, and they that are blind shall see; and the blind shall be led by a way they know not, and the lame shall leap as an hart; and the mighty shall be brought from their seat, and those of low degree exalted.* As this is abode with and walked in, that has wrought these things, a delight in the law of the Lord is known, and a meditating in it day and night.

There is nothing else able to preserve us from lending an ear to the wicked one again, and from walking in the way of sinners again, and to keep down the spirit of exaltation from rising again, but the delighting and meditating in this law. This is the law of the Spirit of Life, which has made free, and is able to preserve us in the freedom whereunto we have attained. All that are strangers to this law, and a meditating in it, they give ear to the wicked, walk in the way of sinners, and sit in the seat of the scornful, let their profession be what it will.

By this one Scripture, all the sects in *Christendom*, who profess the Scriptures to be their rule, may try themselves, whether they are in the state of the *blessed man;* or in the state of the *cursed man.* They need not hire a school Doctor, or learned Rabbi, to give them the meaning of the Scriptures, they being spoken by plain men, and understood only by those who are come to the Spirit.

Those that obey the wicked one lend their ear to him; and those that commit sin, walk in the way of sinners.

XXXIV. It is one of the fundamental doctrines of *Religion*, to believe that God is *omnipresent* and *almighty*; that is, *present at all times and in all places*. This is generally professed and believed among the sects in *Christendom*; but in them, it is no more than a bare profession, a traditional and historical Faith, they not being true witnesses of the same. Herein is the difference betwixt those who do, and those who do not, witness the presence of the Lord, and the almightiness of his power: the first only know the ground and reason why *Moses*, that eminent servant of the Lord, said, *If your presence go not with us, carry us not hence*.

This was the delight of the soul of the righteous in all ages and generations past, and is now; specifically to feel the comfortable presence of the Lord, and to know the light of his countenance lifted up upon them. This makes their hearts more glad than the increase of corn, wine and oil and is better than them all. This was the strength and encouragement of the righteous in all ages, and made them willing to suffer for his name. This carried them through the water and through the fire. This made them sing and rejoice in the prison, and in the stocks, and suffer the spoiling of their goods joyfully. And friends, unless this living presence be felt and enjoyed, known and lived in, we are as weak as other people; and if any lose or depart from it such will become as wicked as others also.

Therefore it is a very precious thing for every individual always to prize the riches of that grace, and the glory of that light, which their minds were at first turned to; which grace and light has led a remnant into the presence chamber, into the banqueting house, where the banner over them is love, and is leading others into the same; and would guide and direct all out of the way of evil, into the way of peace. Oh! the freeness of this love and grace, and the glory of this light which has led a remnant, that have loved it and followed it, into the presence chamber, into the banqueting-house, and to the top of that holy mountain, where the feast of fat things is enjoyed, and the wine well refined drank of; to the right hand, where the rivers of pleasure are. This is free grace and love indeed. This love is stronger than death, and better than life. Oh! the consideration of this love is able to break the heart, to melt the soul before the Lord, and to dissolve it into an holy resignation and pure resolution to walk to the praise, and magnifying of it among the sons and daughters of men, that they may be won and persuaded to accept of its tenders, and follow its leadings; that they may know the pleasantness of its paths, and witness the virtue and operation thereof in their own souls.

XXXV. It is a blessed thing, and a high and heavenly state, for every individual to be witnesses within themselves, that *self is made of no importance*. There is not a people upon the face of the earth, that are in the way to this state, but such whose minds are turned to the light of God within, and are exercised thereby; which alone discovers and makes self manifest in all its appearances, thoughts, ways and imaginations, and leads those that walk in it, to the true self-denial, without which there is no salvation.

For the destruction, loss and misery of all mankind, came in at this door, when he gave heed, credit and importance, to *his own selfish desire, thoughts, reasoning* and *imaginations*; and *would know of himself, be wise of himself*, et cetera. Then the serpent, which spoke of himself, prevailed over him; then he entered into the temptation of the devil, and lost his dwelling-place in paradise. Thus the enemy of man's happiness, under a pretence of advancing him and bettering his state, and making him of some account and importance, drew him into a state of loss and misery. *Self importance* was the first bait of the enemy, and will be his last; therefore watch diligently against it, for herein his power stands, and by this bait, he overcame the first *Adam*; therefore it is a blessed thing to live in the power of the second *Adam*, which makes *self of no importance*. For as sin and the Devil entered and prevailed by reason of some self-importance, so shall he be cast forth and overcome by the Power of God, in all those in whom it makes self of no importance. This is a principal lesson of *Christianity*, which all of necessity, must learn in some measure, before they can be so much as Disciples of Jesus, as himself teaches; *If any man will be my Disciple, he must deny himself, and take up his Cross daily, and follow me.* Denying of self, and taking up the Cross, are inseparable, and must precede Discipleship; yet this state is short of *being a friend of God, and co-heir with Christ, bone of his bone, and flesh of his flesh*; and short of sitting down with him at the right Hand of God in the kingdom of heaven; and as knowing the Son to surrender the kingdom up unto the father, and God to become all in all; short of knowing it meat and drink to do the will of God, and his fruit sweet to their taste, and to sit under his shadow with great delight, glorified with that glory which Christ had with the Father before the world began. In this state, self is made truly of no importance; the first birth is slain, the Serpent's Head is not only bruised, but broken and subdued; the second birth rules, the elder serves the younger, who delights naturally to do the will of God; and it is not a Cross to it, neither is the Cross to be taken up by it; this is the sheep that knows Christ's Voice, and follows him with delight, and a stranger it will not follow.

XXXVI. It is a blessed thing, for people to know *the name of the Lord*. They that know it can trust in it; being as a strong tower unto them, and as a wall of defense, within which the righteous dwell safely, and unto which they fly when *danger does attend*.

It is very precious for people to meet together and wait in this name; such find Jesus, the Savior, in the midst, and know a mounting up as with the wings of an eagle. Such know their bread sure, and their water fails not. Such meet and wait for the better, and not for the worse; they wait not in vain; their strength is renewed; they mount upward, and they know the name of the Lord as precious and as powerful now, as in ages past. They know it as a strong tower indeed, as a safe hiding place, and as precious ointment poured forth, and so they love it, because of the sweet savor thereof, and because they have been made clean, and are preserved by it as virgins; and can say, *your name is as precious ointment poured forth, therefore do the virgins love you.* It was virgin souls in ages past that loved the name of the Lord. It is the virgins now that love the name of the Lord. Those that are joined to any other lovers, cannot love the name of the Lord; though they may pretend much love thereto, their hearts are gone a whoring after other lovers; and though they profess love to the name of the Lord, and take it often into their mouths, and draw near to him with their lips, yet their hearts are gone astray, and they do not depart from iniquity; so though they confess and profess the name of God in words, they deny him in works. Such confessors and professors cause the name of God to be blasphemed amongst the *Heathen*.

This is the name of the Lord, by which he has made known himself unto us, namely, *light*. The pure everlasting light that now shines in our hearts, this is the name of the Lord; for God is *light*, and in him is no *darkness* at all. This is the name of the Lord to us. As we meet in this name, and wait in this name, live together and walk together in this name, we have fellowship with God, and one with another; and we dwell together as in the munitions of rocks, where no evil nor enemy can prevail against us.

In this name, the light, there is no occasion of stumbling; as we love this name and walk in it, we are so far from falling, that we stumble not. It is out of this name the stumbling and falling is, the *evil-doing* is; *he that does evil hates the light, and does not bring his deeds, thoughts and words to it*; so walks, talks, and works in the darkness; not knowing what he said, whither he goes; nor what he does.

All the professors of *Christianity*, and all sects upon the face of the earth, may be tried, measured and judged by this one saying, notwithstanding their talk of loving the name of the Lord, yet if they *do*, or commit, *evil, they hate the light*. This is a universal, infallible truth, let the profession be what it will. If people are found in the evil doing, they hate the light, are enemies to God, loving their evil deeds.

This name of the Lord, the light, which makes all things manifest, and judges every appearance of evil is that which the sect masters in *Christendom* despise and set at naught; and so know not the salvation that is in it; but to them that believe in it, this name is precious, and they have and do witness the sweetness and salvation that is in it, and this is the salvation such have waited for, and do partake of, specifically to be saved from sin, from doing, speaking and thinking of evil, while they dwell in these houses of clay, in these earthen vessels; such have, do and may enjoy the heavenly treasures.

It is a strong delusion indeed, and a gross doctrine of devils, that has overspread the world of mankind in the great night of apostasy, wherein and whereby people are taught and persuaded, *that it is impossible to cease from sin, term of life*: and that, though they continue and remain therein, *yet they shall enjoy the salvation of God after they are dead*, this may very fitly be called the doctrine of devils, and a strong delusion; a state wherein people are given up to believe a lie; seeing as the tree falls so it lies, and there is no repentance in the grave.

This is the happiness of a remnant in this day, that they know the name of the Lord exalted, and set above every name in them, in heaven and in earth, and know every thing, bowing to it, and worshipping before it. Here the King of righteousness is upon his throne; here the righteous bear rule, and the land rejoices; and peace is within their borders.

Meditations & Experiences

This is my testimony, that none can enjoy true peace, but as they witness this name of the Lord exalted in their hearts above every thing; above gold and silver, house and land, wife and children, and self-importance; yes above all heavenly names as well as earthly; and every thought and imagination brought down and subjected to it. There is no other name given under heaven, whereby men can be saved from their enemies within, which are their greatest enemies, but as they witness this name of the Lord exalted in them; specifically his name who said, *I am the light of the world.* This light shows unto man his enemies, and not only so, but destroys them with the breath of his mouth, and the brightness of his coming. Power is in his name, the light, which makes all things manifest, to destroy and expel all that is contrary to it, and redeem mankind from under the power of it. This, a remnant are living witnesses of in this our day, and are ready, in love and good-will, to tell their neighbors, countrymen and acquaintance, what the name of the Lord, through their loving of it, has done for their souls; that they may be persuaded to embrace it, and come to experience the like great salvation.

Great is the knowledge that is broken forth in our hearts and understandings, and glorious is the light of that day that now shines; what then remains, but that all that have received this knowledge, do walk answerable to it; and that all, in whom this light shines, abide in it and love it; so a vain thought cannot arise, nor an idle word be spoken, nor an evil deed be done, but they are judged and condemned by it.

This light that judges every appearance of evil, is a day of judgment, wherein men give an account for every idle word they speak.

XXXVII. It is a certain truth, testified by the apostle, when he said; *great is the mystery of godliness.*

And this is one of the great mysteries that *God is very near unto the sons and daughters of men;* many of them are very far from him. God is in the world, but the world knows him not; and God, who is light, shines in darkness, but the darkness does not comprehend him. He is in men, and they live, move and have their being by him; yet they are without him, without God in the world; strangers to him, though he is not far from every one.

In this stands the happiness of a remnant that they know God not only near them, and in them, but also they know themselves near unto him; he dwelling in them, and they in him. These are they that enjoy the effect of that blessed prayer of Christ Jesus, *that they may be one, as thou Father, and I am one; I in them, and thou in me*. This is the blessed unity and heavenly fellowship, which the primitive *Christians* were witnesses of, when they said, *truly our fellowship is with the Father and with his Son*.

This is a state worth waiting to feel and enjoy. It is more than words can express, and is the end of all words and declarations. None are to sit down short of this state. This is the end of the race, and the mark of the high calling of God in Christ Jesus. Here is the *seeing eye to eye*, and the *talking with God as a man talks with his friend*. Here is the *seeing as you are seen*, and the *knowing as you are known*. Here is the *walking with God as* Enoch *did*; and here is the *talking with him, as* Abraham, Moses *and the prophets did*. Here is the *coming of the Lord to the last supper known, where the delicacies are prepared, and the wine well refined*. Here is the *fruit of the vine drank new in the kingdom of God*. Here is the *marriage union, where the water is turned into wine;* where the *bride and the bridegroom rejoice together;* where the *tears are wiped of all faces;* where there is *no crying, nor pain, death nor sorrow*. Here *death is swallowed up in victory, darkness in light, fear in love, in which is no torment*. Here is the truth of that saying witnessed, *love castes out fear*. This is the love, which is greater than *faith*, greater than hope, the end of *faith* and *hope*, and remains when they are gone. This was the first, and will be the last; blessed are all that dwell and abide in it; no evil can enter their dwellings.

XXXVIII. It is the blessing of all blessings, to know *the low valley*, where the *green pastures* are, where the *safe feeding is*, where none can *make afraid*; the feeding in this low valley, where the fatness of the Lord's house is, where the greenness and safety is, where the ravenous beast cannot come. The feeding here is more than words; it is the end of all words and declarations. It is the end of the Lord, in sending his messengers of the everlasting gospel among us; it is their crown and rejoicing to find us feeding in this low valley, where the idol shepherds and their flocks cannot partake with us; they know not the way that leads thereto.

The very remembrance of the time wherein the call of the Lord reached us, and called us out of the holes of the rocks, and of the high hills and barren mountains, into the valley of *Jehoshaphat*, where the pleading with all flesh with fire and sword is, and where the judgment is known, by which *Zion* is redeemed. I say, the remembrance of this day is very precious to a remnant, and the ministration thereof was glorious in its time: but this is more glorious, to dwell in this low valley, where the green pastures of life and salvation are fed on, where the growing is unto the stature and fullness of Christ; where no fear is; where the cause of it is taken away; where the pleasant rivers run; where the tranquility of mind, peace and full satisfaction is enjoyed. This is the blessing of blessings, and the portion of a remnant in this the day of the Lord's love, and exceeding riches and kindness; and those that truly enjoy the least measure of it, esteem it above all the world, because they well know, that all things therein are not sufficient to purchase the least dram thereof.

XXXIX. It is a very blessed thing for every individual, within themselves, to feel and know the Spirit of God bear witness with their spirits, that *they are true waiters upon and worshippers of him.*

Many glorious things, according to the testimony of the patriarchs, prophets, and apostles, do accompany those that wait upon the Lord, and are enjoyed by them. One could say, *they that wait upon the Lord, shall lack no good thing.* This one sentence is sufficient to try all the pretenders to wait upon the Lord in *Christendom*, who profess a waiting upon him in *Ordinances*, yet are found lacking *the good thing.* Poverty, blindness and nakedness, leanness of soul and barrenness of heart, are their daily companions; so instead of lacking no good thing, they lack all good things relating to their inward man. Another could say, *they that wait upon the Lord, their strength shall be renewed, they should mount upward as upon* eagles' *wings, walk without weariness, run without fainting.* No bare formal professor in *Christendom* can be a living witness of these things; such may infallibly conclude, that they are deceived and mistaken in the cause, when the effect does not follow; for this is the testimony of truth to all the sects in *Christendom*, and the diverse worshippers elsewhere in the world; let them profess what they will, yes though it be the truth itself, if they enjoy not the good things, if they feel not their strength renewed, so as to run without weariness, and walk without fainting; if they grow not from grace to grace, from knowledge to knowledge; if they increase not with the increase of God in the inward man; they deceive their own souls with a vain, dead, fruitless profession, which profits nothing, but will vanish like smoke in the day of the Lord.

XL. It is a precious thing to be witnesses of the presence of Jesus in the midst, *as a peaceable Savior,* for those that know him so, live, abide, and walk in him, are of the number of those which need no repentance. Indeed, it is a high and heavenly state to come to this degree of knowledge. None come higher, but such who have first known him as a judge and reprover, as a refiner with consuming fire, and as an overcomer of all their enemies in them; the great dragon bound, the mouth of the bottomless pit stopped, and standing upon the sea of glass mingled with fire; being witnesses of victory over the beast and his image, and over the mark and number of his name. These are they that come to sing the song of *Moses* and the *Lamb*, not only upon the banks of salvation, but in the midst of *Jerusalem*, which comes down from God out of Heaven; and before the throne of the Lamb, who is the light thereof, and has redeemed them from the earth, and has saved them with a great salvation.

XLI. That which was lost is now found; the *precious pearl* that was hid in the field, a remnant in this age has dug deep and found it, and many rejoice in the sight and knowledge of it; but let all understand this, that it is not sufficient to find the heavenly treasure, the precious pearl, but to purchase it and possess it; specifically by selling all, parting with all for it. Nothing in our hearts, nothing in our esteem, must stand in competition with it; all must be laid down for it. It is a true saying spoken by Jesus, *If any man love any thing more than me, he is not worthy of me.* He alone must reign and rule, and have the government in our hearts. We must know him to be the foundation, corner and top-stone, elect and precious.

It is not sufficient to know him as a little stone cut out of the mountain without hands, smiting at the feet of all imagery; but to know him grown and increased to an exceeding great mountain, and to fill the earth, and to become all in all; to know every thing, to bow at his name; every high thought, every imagination, every vile affection, selfish will, and desire denied, brought down and subdued into obedience to the name, to the Power of God. This is the blessed state all, that have not only the knowledge of the field where the pearl is hid, but have also dug deep therein, and found it, are to wait for and experience; and not to sit down short of this in the sight, knowledge, and profession of the precious pearl, but to purchase, inherit, possess, and enjoy it; that they may be able to say, *My beloved is mine, and I am his*; here is the feeding among the lilies, where there is neither toiling nor spinning.

XLII. That which makes a people blessed, above all the families of the earth, is, that they in their solemn assemblies, and at all times, are sensible of that power, that makes *self of no importance, even self in its innocence*; for such a *self* Christ had, which was humbled, and made obedient to the death of the cross; and this is the way to an high and heavenly exaltation, which as people come to walk in, as the captain of our salvation did, the serpent that beguiled in paradise, by drawing mankind into self-exaltation and self-importance, cannot, nor shall ever prevail against them.

For the worship which this Power has led us to, begins not when our solemn assemblies begin, neither does it end when we part, but is in that which is without beginning or end, specifically in the Spirit, and in the truth, into which the deceiver cannot come.

It is a precious state, a high and heavenly condition, to witness self made of no importance, and to have unity with that Power that has made it so. They that remain and abide in it, no temptation can prevail against. So the whole duty of those that are come to the knowledge of this Power, and to have faith in it, is always to cleave unto it with their whole hearts, and to fix their minds upon it; that in the midst of all temptations and trials, they may witness deliverance and salvation by it, and such shall never miss of the same; for it is said, when Christ was tempted, after the temptation was over, *Angels ministered unto him*. The same is witnessed now by a remnant, in measure, Praises to the Lord! Such experience the blessedness that attends enduring temptation, and do magnify the Power, over the power of the evil one; and walk to the praise and glory of it; and herein they differ from others; a talk and profession only, differs not, but a living in the sense and obedience of that Power, which makes self of no importance.

Self became of some repute, when temptation at first entered mankind; the giving credit to the Devil's saying, *you shall be as Gods*, et cetera, begot a selfish hope of a selfish gain; so being deceived, a vain desire of self-importance, sprang and increased, disobedience to the command and Power of God, and a selfish hope and confidence were immediate companions in the beginning, which all the children of the light, that are come to a dwelling place in paradise, are to watch against, lest, as the serpent beguiled *Eve*, he beguile them.

XLIII. The night is far spent, darkness is past, and the *true Light now shines*, the *day of God is dawned*, the *daystar is risen in the hearts of thousands*.

This state and knowledge is very glorious in its time, and is more than all the bare professors in *Christendom* know and understand. But that which we are to wait for, and press after, is a further thing, or a knowledge of the same thing, in a greater degree of glory, *specifically to know the Sun of Righteousness arise, with healing under his wings.* This is more precious, and a greater degree of knowledge, specifically to experience the healing virtue of the Sun of Righteousness, this ministration succeeds that of discovering, reproving, convincing, smiting, correcting, and wounding; this binds up and heals, this comforts and consolates the soul, refreshes and gladdens the heart, and ministers the joy of God's salvation. To live in the sense and feeling of this healing virtue, this saving and preserving Power, not only in our solemn assemblies, but at other times, is very precious. This cures all diseases and infirmities, and takes away, disperses and removes the cause of hurts and wounds; the cause of smiting, convincing, and reproving; and preserves from falling into the same again; so as we live and abide in it, we can never err, nor ever need *reproof, smiting,* or *wounding.* It is the world that lies in that state, where the Spirit of God convinces for evil, reproves, smites and wounds for transgression; but to us salvation is now nearer than when we first believed, and the great day of salvation is come; the maker up of the breach, and the healer of nations is come. Blessed are all that do experience the healing virtue thereof, and the blessed effect of his appearing with heavenly healing under his wings; so that they can say, their *soul-sickness is cured,* and their *wounds not only bound up, but healed,* and *they cleansed and made sound, both in soul, body and spirit.* Such are fitted and prepared to have their conversation with God in heaven, and sit there in the enjoyment of the light of his countenance, which is better than the increase of all other things.

It is the taste of the rivers of pleasure that are at his right hand, and of the wine in his kingdom, that engages those that drink thereof, to wait to partake more and more of the same. It is *because of the savor of his good ointment, that the virgins love him.*

If there was no good savor, if there was not something felt and witnessed, of greater worth and value than the treasures and pleasures this world can afford, the souls of the righteous would not long after it and become sick of love, nor be encouraged to wait to enjoy the increase and abounding of it.

In this stands our happiness, *daily to experience and partake* of the virtue of this healing, saving and preserving Power, to feel our hearts and minds joined to it, united to it, become one with it. Herein is our everlasting blessedness; and this truly distinguishes such from all the bare professors in *Christendom*, specifically as they walk and abide in this blessed light, and sun of righteousness, that is risen and now shines, and in the witnessing the healing virtue thereof.

XLIV. It is a precious state to be of a *tender spirit*, of a *soft heart*, prepared *to wait upon the Lord*. Such are in a capacity to know when *good comes*; they are not like the parched heath, nor barren desert, but like the tender herb; they sensible of the dews from heaven, and of the gentle rain that falls, and the fruitful showers that descend upon them; they can feel the droppings down of divine love, and sprout forth and sing for joy in the sense thereof. But those whose hearts are stony, and whose spirits are hard, they cannot taste and see how good the Lord is; such are not prepared to wait upon the Lord, nor to draw near unto him, and partake of his divine refreshments, neither have they the sacrifice wherein his soul delights, which is *a broken heart and contrite spirit*. Oh! it is a blessed thing for people to meet together, and wait in the sense and feeling of the tendering Power of the Lord; specifically that Power that sought us out, and gathered us in the beginning, to have our hearts exercised in this tendering Power, which is now with us, and attends upon us, for our good and preservation. This is that which makes us and our solemn assemblies differ from all the bare professors of *Christianity*. They that so meet and so wait, sit as at the table of the Lord, feeding upon that which is meat indeed, and drinking of the wine that he has prepared, feeding upon life itself, and the substance itself. This is better than to sit at the table of princes; all the banquets and delicacies of the earth are not to be compared to it. As every mind and heart keeps in the sense of the tendering Power of the Lord, they are living witnesses of the preciousness of it. Here none can forget the loving-kindness of the Lord, nor let his benefits slip out of their minds; but are in a capacity to praise and magnify him for all his mercies and heavenly blessings, and wonderful kindnesses and deliverances that he has wrought for them, specifically as great as for any people in any age of the world. They can say, *he has not only brought them out of* Egypt, *through the Red Sea and wilderness*, but also *into the good Land*, and has *divided their inheritance unto them*; and they can say, *their lot is fallen into a good place*; feeling the flowing of the milk and honey, they eat and drink, and praise the Lord in the sense of all his mercies, blessings and salvation, that they are accompanied and surrounded with.

Meditations & Experiences

This is the mystery of our fellowship, and the bond of our unity, as our minds and hearts are exercised in the tendering Power of the Lord, especially in our solemn meetings and waiting together upon him, as every one keeps close unto this, and are united unto it. Oh! this is a precious state, herein stands our blessed unity and fellowship, herein we are strong, specifically as *Mount Zion*, as a three-fold cord that cannot easily be broken. As we keep and abide in this, the gates of Hell cannot prevail against us, no evil can hurt us. In this stands our joy and preservation in our meetings, and in our partings, in all times and places, as we feel our hearts and minds in unity with the Spirit of the Lord; then not convinced, reproved and condemned by it; but justified and commended. This is sweet and precious indeed, as all that are in it know full well.

XLV. It is he that stays at home, *that divides the spoil of his enemies*. It is he that stays at home, *that obtains the blessing*. The wanderer and hunter do not: he toils and wearies himself, and sells his birthright.

It is the retired mind, the staid mind, the mind whose loins are girded with the girdle of truth, staid upon the Lord, *that receives the blessing*, and *knows a being kept in perfect peace*, according as it was witnessed of old; *you will keep him in perfect peace, whose mind is staid upon you*. This to enjoy, is the mark of the high calling of God in Christ Jesus, which we have been and are called unto, specifically to enjoy perfect peace, *to be entire, lacking nothing*. This to enjoy, is the end, sum and substance of the *Christian* religion.

It is those that are witnesses of a retiredness and a staidness of their minds upon the Lord that inherit substance. It is those that have known the candle of the Lord lighted in them; and have swept their own house, and found the piece of silver, and that rejoice therefore.

This heavenly light that now shines, discovers the vanity and emptiness of all things below the Sun; and by the same, our minds have been redeemed from under them, and are become living witnesses, that neither all the treasures, pleasures, opinions and religions that are in the world, nor the bare profession of truth itself, was able or sufficient to stay or satisfy our souls: We have found them all prove a very vanity and vexation of spirit.

For the soul of man is in itself more excellent, more noble, and of greater value than all these things, and is superior to them all. The lesser cannot satisfy or fill the greater; nor that which is inferior, ignoble and less excellent, stay or satisfy that which is superior or more worthy, noble and excellent in nature, capacity and being. As the soul of mankind is above all created sublunary beings, therefore *all things under the sun, instead of food and satisfaction unto it, prove vanity, emptiness and vexation of spirit.*

So blessed is the remembrance of that day and time, wherein our minds were turned to the true everlasting light that now shines, which has discovered the vanity and nothingness of all things below the sun, and has redeemed the children thereof from under them all, up unto him who is in them, through them, and above them all, God blessed for ever. And brings into the one true everlasting universal worship, which stands in the Spirit and in the truth. Here God who is light, and dwells in the light, is bowed unto, worshipped and obeyed.

XLVI. It is a blessed thing, and those are the people who have attained to a heavenly state, who can experimentally witness and seal to the truth of that ancient testimony in the Holy Scriptures, *darkness is past, and the true light now shines.*

I say it is a blessed thing to witness the truth of this or to be able to say *darkness is past.* Those that have known what it is to dwell in darkness and to work and travel in the land thereof, and have been surrounded therewith, and encompassed with the thick mists and fogs in the dark region of the shadow of death; such can remember that their steps were made in solitary places; and their habitation as where *dragons, owls and bats were their companions*; and therein were stumbling and groping, like blind men for the wall; these have been in this state, who are come to know redemption and deliverance from it, and can say in truth, *that darkness is past, and the true light now shines in and unto them*; these can say, it is a blessed state indeed; and that it is more to witness and experience the truth of these three words, *darkness is past,* than only to hear and read thousands of good words. There is much in the words; those that know *darkness is past and gone,* are come to the everlasting day of God, to the rising of the glorious sun of righteousness, which has caused the very shadows of death to flee away; and they know the very womb in which is, and has been bred and generated, all the evil and wickedness that comes forth in the world of mankind, made barren, removed and vanished away. They are come to the springing of that day, and to the arising of that sun, that disperses all the mists and fogs, clouds and errors that did encompass them about, and made them to walk in the shadow of death. Their hearts are made to rejoice in the feeling and enjoyment thereof, their eyes become satisfied, with seeing the glory of the true light that now shines, and they find their hearts engaged to walk in the same; not only to profess and talk of it, but to *walk in it*; and become not only children of it, but young men, fathers and elders in it. *Walking in the light*, implies no less than being led and guided by it, than bringing every thought, word and deed to it, *to be tried*, not only in our solemn meetings and assemblies, but at other times; in our affairs, dealings and converse among men, specifically in our common occasions; and as all are found herein, they are in the true worship of God, whether together or asunder.

XLVII. They are true and faithful sayings testified of old, *that there remains a rest, and the believer enters into it*; and *he that is entered into this rest, has ceased from his own works, as God did from his*. This is the substance and antitype of the *Jews'* sabbath; and this rest is inward and spiritual, specifically a stay and rest for the soul, wherein that blessed state, spoken of in old time, is witnessed, *namely, You will keep him in perfect peace, whose mind is staid upon you*. This is a blessed state indeed, *to be kept in perfect peace*; those that know an entrance into this rest, and abide in it, know a ceasing from their own works, from following their own thoughts, and doing their own will: such keep holy day to the Lord; and do know that the day of the Lord, long spoken and prophesied of, is come, and that the glorious light thereof now shines.

This is the day of the great Sabbath, in which Christ stands up as a teacher of his people, and they hear and understand his voice, and follow him, and shut their ear against the many voices that are in the world. This is the teacher we have been directed to from the beginning. We have not been called to a noise or sound of words, nor to a bare profession; but to inherit substance, to enjoy rest, specifically that rest which has been prepared of old for the people of God, *and which does remain*, and is very glorious, as those that have entered into it can witness; and this is my experience and testimony, that none can enter into this rest, but as they know a ceasing from their own works, their own willing, running and thinking, and every thought brought into the obedience of Christ; no further than this is effected, can any entrance be witnessed by any into this rest that is *prepared*, and that does *remain*, let the peoples' talk and profession be what it will.

XLVIII. This is a great truth, that where *a bridle to the tongue is not known, and a chain to the will, affections, lusts and passions witnessed*, the religion of such is *vain*, though such may talk of rest and peace, yet they enjoy none.

John the divine *saw an angel come down from heaven, having the key of the bottomless-pit and a great chain in his hand, who laid hold upon the dragon, that old serpent, which is the devil and Satan, and bound him.* This every individual is to see and know effected in the revelation of God, before they can witness an entrance into, and a sitting down in that rest which is glorious, and which the light of this glorious day leads the children thereof into: so it is precious to wait upon the Lord, who dwells in the light, and leads the children thereof into the enjoyment of rest.

XLIX. Certainly it was the joy and delight of the righteous in all ages, to draw *near unto the Lord with their hearts*; to be *inward with him in their minds*; and it is the joy and delight of the righteous in this age, who, by drawing near unto the Lord, experience the truth of that testimony, *those that draw near unto the Lord, the Lord will draw near unto them*, and are witnesses of his heavenly presence, and partake of the joy of his salvation, having their conversation in heaven, where God dwells; and walk with him as *Enoch, Abraham, Moses*, and the prophets did. This is witnessed by a remnant in this age, as in ages past; for the day of life and salvation is come, and the blessed way that leads thereto is known, and evidently made manifest to thousands in this our native country, and island of the *gentiles*, on whom the glory of the Lord is risen.

It is a blessed thing to know the way of life and salvation, but it is more blessed, and a greater degree of happiness, for every individual, to whom it has appeared, to know themselves fitted and prepared, by walking in the light thereof, *to possess and inherit the same*. This is that which is worthy to be waited for, and is the blessed end of all holy writing, reading, preaching and believing, specifically to possess the thing read, written and preached of. Such as are taught of the Lord, and established in righteousness, not only know it, and profess it, but are established in it. This is the mark of the high calling, which all that are but in the way that leads thereto, are to press after, that they may come to the enjoyment thereof.

It is the tasting and seeing how good the Lord is, that raises and quickens desires to enjoy him, and more and more engages to draw near unto him, and to wait upon him. It is the tasting of the streams of the river of life and pleasure that is at the right Hand of God, that alone renews strength; and such only are witnesses of the truth of that saying, they *that wait upon the Lord shall renew their strength, and mount upward as upon the wings of an eagle, run without weariness, and walk without fainting*, specifically in the way of God's commandments with delight; being become more natural and pleasant so to do, than ever it was to do the contrary.

This is the blessed state and privilege of many, to draw so near unto the Lord, that as they not only taste and see the goodness of the Lord, but are also filled and satisfied with the renewing of strength, divine refreshments, and heavenly consolation in their souls, whereby they are made more and more in love with him, and engaged continually to wait upon him. And in this stands the happiness and preservation of all, specifically as the eye of their minds is kept looking unto the Lord, and waiting upon him, specifically as the eye of the maid is upon the hand of her mistress, and much more. Where this tasting, seeing, drawing, and waiting is, wanting, weakness, weariness, and fainting abounds, and the enemy of their soul prevails, let the talk and profession of religion be what it will.

L. It is a blessing, yes, the blessing of all blessings, for every individual to know and feel within themselves, that *the Spirit of God bears witness with their spirits*, that *they are the sons and daughters of God*, that *they are begotten by him to a lively hope;* whereby *they purify themselves even as he is pure*, and that they are *Christians* indeed, *Israelites* indeed, in whom is no guile. This I say is the blessing of all blessings, for every one to have the Spirit of God to witness those things unto them; and this is precious to wait for and enjoy; for he that has called us is holy, harmless and without guile; so as we follow and obey him, we shall be like him, as the primitive *Christians* were, who said, *we know that when he does appear, we shall be like him.* This testimony of the Spirit of God is more than a thousand witnesses. It was the only comforter of the righteous in all ages past, and is the same now.

It is good to mind the Spirit and its testimony, so as to become spiritually minded; then life and peace is known, and death and trouble vanishes away, and the truth of that saying is witnessed, *to be spiritually minded is life and peace, but to be carnally minded is death.*

Of a truth, the Spirit of grace and truth is come, and many are living witnesses of its appearance and power, not only to reprove and convince, but to comfort and console, those that have and do wait for its appearance, and are in love therewith, and have their ear open to its teaching, and their minds and hearts exercised in it. In this stands the everlasting joy, peace, comfort and consolation of the righteous, even as they continually learn of the Spirit of grace, and are witnesses of the leading of it and guidance of it, out of all evil into all good. As they keep in the sense and exercise of this Spirit of grace, they excel all the bare professors in *Christendom*. This alone makes them differ from them, even as they grow in spirit, from one degree of grace unto another, from knowledge to knowledge, from faith to faith, from strength to strength, from children to young men, from young men to elders and fathers, even to the stature and fullness of Christ, having his mind; *doing always that which pleases God*. Such are sons of God without rebuke, and are able to say as some of old, did *namely, we can do nothing against the Truth*. This is an high and heavenly state indeed, which all are to wait for and press after, which is possible to be attained unto, even in this age, as in ages past; and such can say, *greater is he that is in us, than he that is in the world*; and are daily witnesses of his strength, in preserving them out of the evil of the world, though they live and labor in it, and daily converse with the children thereof.

This is that which keeps us a living virtuous people, even as we abide in him, increase and grow in him, who at first appeared unto us, and unto whom our minds were at first directed. Herein we shall be preachers of righteousness, lights of the world, and as the salt of the earth indeed.

LI. It is a precious thing to *wait, walk and dwell in the light*, even in that which makes all things manifest; and those that wait and walk in it, are led by it to the rising of the Sun specifically the everlasting Sun of righteousness, whose glory, light and virtue, does as really disperse and drive away the vain thoughts, dark imaginations, fogs, clouds and mists of ignorance and darkness within, as the outward sun does expel, extinguish, and cause the fogs, mists and darkness to vanish away outwardly: *this many are witnesses of.*

The very remembrance of the first discovery of truth under this name, *light*, in this our age, is very precious. The truth is but one, but it has many names; and this name, *light*, to a remnant, is very excellent. Many righteous men and prophets, in former ages, foretold of the glory of this day or *light* that now shines, and prophesied of its breaking forth unto a people that sat in darkness, and that were covered with the shadow of the night, and dwelt in the region of death. We see the fulfilling of these things; for we sat in darkness and wandered in desolate places, and were encompassed with the region and shadow of death. Oh! how sweet was the light when it first sprang unto us, and caused us to see over the tops of the high mountains of darkness, and discovered unto us the secret chambers of imagery, and the hidden things of darkness, and guided our feet out of the mire and clay, and set them at liberty to walk in that path which leads out of the way of death and darkness.

This is that manifestation of light by which all these things are effected, to which our minds were at first turned; which light judges every appearance of evil, and leads all, that walk in it, out of the same. This is the path-way, that not only leads into innocence, but preserves in it; for there is a possibility in this age as of old, that people may lose a good state, be tempted out of innocence and a virgin's state, after they have attained unto it. This made *Paul* exhort those he wrote to, *to beware lest the serpent beguiled them as he did* Eve. *How was that?* why, draw or allure them out of innocence, out of harmlessness and a sinless state, into sin or breach of God's commandments, to the loss of Paradise. This he has done, and may do again, people may lose a good state, yes, their place in Paradise, if not watchful; therefore good is it to wait and watch in the light, which not only leads into the garden of God again, and brings to the tree of life, and gives right to eat thereof, but also preserves in the same; discovers and gives dominion over the tempter, and keeps from falling into the temptation.

It is no wonder to us, why the old enemy of mankind rages against the truth, under this name, *light*; and that he gives it so many opprobrious and despicable names, that people might not regard it, nor believe in it, *as it is*; knowing that it undermines his kingdom of darkness, and discovers him and all his works, and destroys them also. We are witnesses of the Power and virtue of faith in the *light*, that it is able to break all the chains of darkness, and deliver out of the fetters of death and Hell; and we also know, that there is not any other way or means under heaven appointed of God, that is able to effect this work. All other ways, means and inventions of men, are not able to break one link of the chains of darkness. 'Tis faith in Christ, the *light*, which reproves the world of sin. Though this light shines in the world, in wicked men, in darkness, yet they having not faith in it, believing not in it, as that in which God dwells, they never know the saving power and virtue thereof; yet its reproving and condemning power such shall not escape.

LII. It is a blessed thing, for people *to know the name of the Lord*, even as some in ages past knew it, and have left their knowledge and experience upon record; who could say and witness, *that the name of the Lord* was a *buckler*, as a *shield*, as a *tower* of *defense*, yes, as a *strong tower*, into which the righteous fled and were safe. It is very precious for people so to know the name of the Lord, and to meet together in it; such are in capacity to enjoy, possess and inherit all the *blessings* that ever were promised, and to avoid and escape all the *curses* that were ever threatened.

The glorious light of the gospel, that now shines, is the *name of the Lord*, whereby he has made himself manifest to us in this our day and age. As we wait together, and walk in this name, we are witnesses and experiencers of the fulfilling of that promise, *where two or three are met together in my name, there am I in the midst*; such know their teacher, their Savior, in the midst, and their eye is towards him, and their ear open to his voice, who is a teacher, one of a thousand, who teaches to profit indeed. Many that have learned of him, can say, *they soon became wiser than all their former teachers*. Thus to hear and learn of him, is the blessed end of all preaching, hearing and believing; and of all the ordinances, ministrations, dispensations and appointments of God, ever since the fall of man, even *to hear and obey the voice of the Son of God*, who is light, and dwells in the light, wherein the righteous in all ages had fellowship with God, and one with another.

To know this *name*, is more than talk and a bare profession. To know it as a safe hiding place, a sure rock, and tower of defense when the enemy assaults, when floods of temptations attend, when arrows fly by night, and cease not in the day: when storms descend, and winds blow. This was and is the blessed end of the knowledge of the *name* of the Lord in all ages, to save and preserve them that *have* it, from all dangers that attend them at all times and in all places, from the enemy of their souls, that his fiery darts may not hurt them, nor his floods drown them, nor the storms and winds overthrow them, nor the enemies of their house prevail against them.

This was the reason why those that knew it, compared it to a *strong tower*, et cetera. They often meditated in it, and thought upon the name of the Lord, and thereby found strength *to abstain from every appearance of evil*, and to resist the devil in all his attempts. This is a happy state indeed, which those only that know the name of the Lord, and can trust in it, do enjoy.

Meditations & Experiences

By this may all the bare professors of all the various names in *Christendom*, so called, be proved and tried; who talk much, and profess much, of the name of the Lord, but do *not depart from iniquity, do not cease from evil*, do not know his name as a *strong tower*, to save and preserve them from the strength and power of the enemy of their souls; so notwithstanding their great profession of the name of the Lord, they do *not depart from iniquity*; and though they take his name into their mouths, they *hate to be reformed by him*; which is a great abomination to the Lord, and stinks in his nostrils. For this I testify in the name of the Lord, that all people upon the face of the earth, let their name and sort of religion be what it will, who profess the name of the Lord, and are found in *evil doing*, their profession is vain, and their religions a lie. In sin they live, and in sin they will die, unless they come to know that repentance which is never to be repented of; till which, they can never come to know the name of the Lord as a *strong tower, buckler or shield;* but are led captive and ensnared by the enemy of their souls, even at his pleasure.

LIII. In this stands our blessedness and everlasting happiness, as our eye is kept always looking to Jesus, the author and finisher of our faith, and not only to know him the *author* the *beginner* of faith, but the *finisher*, and *ender* also; to know the end of faith, which is *the salvation of our souls;* such know salvation nearer than when they first believed. It is a blessed thing to have and know that faith which Jesus is the author of, the least measure of which, is very precious and very powerful; though it be but as a grain of mustard-seed, it removes mountains, and does wonderful things. Many are living witnesses in this age, as in ages past, of the power of faith specifically in the beginning of its work; but it is an higher state to know the end of it, the finishing of it, to know the work thereof done; to know the heart purified by it, and the victory over the world obtained; the wicked one subdued and overcome, brought down and destroyed. This is a blessed state indeed, and that which all are to wait for, press after and witness. The only way to attain it, is always to look to Jesus, to keep the eye of the mind toward him, and the ear open to him, who alone teaches to profit, *even in silence*, when no word is spoken outwardly. This is the blessed end of the ministry and ministers of truth the Lord has sent amongst us, and of all preaching, writing and printing, specifically that every one's eye might be turned to Jesus, always looking to him who has begun the good work, and who alone is able to finish it.

LIV. It is a blessed state, to *be as a stranger and pilgrim on the earth*, and to be able to say in truth, as some of old did, *we have here no continuing city, but we seek one to come*. I say, this is a blessed state; but it is more blessed to find the city sought for, to know the heavenly city to be come, to know the heavenly *Jerusalem* come down from above, from God out of heaven, and to be a citizen of it; such dwell in a quiet habitation; such are redeemed from the earth, who dwell in this heavenly city, where no unclean thing can enter; they dwell not upon the earth, neither do they inhabit the dark corners thereof, where the woe and misery is, as it is written, *woe to them that dwell upon the earth: woe to the inhabitants of the earth, for the Devil is come down amongst you*, et cetera. Oh! let none that talk of, and profess themselves citizens of the heavenly *Jerusalem*, be found inhabiters of the earth! But let all travel *Zion-ward*, until they come to dwell therein, and become free citizens thereof, who are not fellow citizens with the saints in light, who dwell not within the gates thereof. Oh! press forward to the same, that a sitting down in the kingdom you may witness. This is the end of our pilgrimage; the end of seeking a city that will continue, whose builder and Maker is God, who is worshipped in this city in the Spirit, in the truth, and has everlasting praise from all the inhabitants thereof.

The outward *Jew*, the outward *Jerusalem*, the outward *Temple*, the outward furniture thereof, and the worships and worshippers therein, were shadows, figures and types of these things. *Jerusalem* was the place of worship, and all were to repair there to worship, to make their offerings, and to offer their sacrifices; and wherever the people were, when they prayed or worshipped, they were to turn their faces towards the city of *Jerusalem*. To be witnesses of the coming down of the heavenly city *Jerusalem*, and a being fellow citizens of the saints in light, is the antitype and substance of those things, and of all the blessed promises relating thereunto, and is that which all are to wait for, who have not attained thereto, but are in the way thereof.

LV. It is a true saying, recorded in the holy Scriptures, that the *word is near, in the mouth, and in the heart; none need to ascend or descend to fetch it down, or bring it up*. This was the word of Faith, preached and believed by the primitive *Christians*, and is now again preached and believed in by a remnant in this age. Blessed are all those that know, experience and abide in the same, that hear and obey the voice and teachings thereof, that are learning of it, not only when they meet together in one place, but at other times and places, in their common occasions to lend their ear unto it, and receive its instruction. Such assuredly will be made wise unto salvation. Such will not be always learning, and never educated; neither will they remain laden with sin, nor be led about by diverse lusts, but will witness the powerful salvation of God, through faith in the word, *which is quick, sharp and powerful*; quick to teach and instruct in all that is good; and to reprove and condemn all that is evil; and sharp and powerful to cut down and destroy that which did formerly load with sin, and led into the things that are evil.

The hearing and obeying this word of life, this in speaking word of God, that is near in the mouth and in the heart, is the only ground of all true learning and knowledge; and all that despise the voice of it, and shut their ears against the teachings of it and have not faith in it, though they may be furnished with all the academic learning in the world, and be diligent hearkeners to the voice of men and books, yet will they remain strangers to, and ignorant of the pure sanctifying, satisfying wisdom, and peaceable salvation of God, and under the burden and power of sin, under the command of their lusts, wills and passions.

The lack of faith in the word and Power of God within, and the neglect of hearing the still small voice thereof, is the ground and cause of all ignorance, errors, darkness and confusion among men, of all sects and sorts of religion upon the face of the whole earth.

LVI. It is a precious thing to *have faith*, and to *be always looking unto Jesus the author and finisher of it*; and to *be growing and increasing in it, from one degree unto another*. They are the blessed people who wait, walk and live together in this faith, which Jesus is the author of, and is the same which was once delivered to the saints; being the *gift of God*, and not of man. The least measure of which is very powerful, though but as a grain of mustard-seed, it is able to remove mountains; and all that know the growing and increase of it, and persevere therein, come to know *Jesus* not only the *author*, but the *finisher of faith*; not only the *beginner*, but the *ender* of it; for faith has an end, specifically the salvation of the soul; and all that attain to that end can rejoice in the salvation of God, which is come nearer unto them than when they first believed.

Let all the sects in *Christendom*, who talk of having faith in God, try and examine *what their faith has done for them*. If it has not removed mountains of darkness and ignorance; if it has not purified their hearts; if it has not given them victory over the world, saved them out of the evil thereof, enabled them to please God, to live unto him, and to find acceptance with him; if they know not these things wrought in them and for them, they may infallibly conclude *their faith is dead*, and is none of that faith which is the gift of God, once delivered to, and received by the primitive saints, which Jesus was the author of; but is a faith of their own making, and is like the faith of devils, who *believe and tremble*; the only fruit and effect of the faith of devils and wicked men.

LVII. It is a blessed thing to know and *witness a meeting and waiting together in the name of Jesus*; such as meet in this name, and know Jesus the peaceable Savior in the midst of them, know the heavenly adorning of a meek and quiet spirit, the Prince of peace, and his peaceable government, the Lamb upon the throne, the righteous bearing rule, the land rejoicing, and heavenly peace in their borders.

It is the true waiters and meeters in this name that enjoy all the blessings promised. It is they that know their strength, faith and confidence in God renewed; their wisdom and knowledge increased with the increase of God; they know the light to shine more and more unto a perfect day, as was witnessed of old, *the just man's path is a shining light, that shines more and more unto a perfect day*.

But before this city is known, *Jerusalem* must be searched as with candles, even *Jerusalem* the chosen beloved city, and every inhabitant of it; and the blessed end of searching, is to cleanse and purify it. Judgment begins at the house of God, to purge away and sweep out all that does defile, and to lay waste *Babylon* the city of confusion, the mystery of impurity. These things are to be known and experienced in every individual, even *Jerusalem* searched and cleansed, and *Babylon* wasted and destroyed, and the increase of the kingdom of Heaven within, the Power, light, and glory thereof shining more and more within. As in this name we meet and abide, we feel the kingdom come, and the will of God done; and whatsoever we ask in this name, we receive, according to Christ's promise; for we have not been called to a sound of words, to figures, types and shadows, nor to depend upon the lips of others, though enabled to make long declarations of the truth itself; but to inherit substance, to feel Jesus the truth in the midst, the tree of life in the midst, and to eat of the fruit thereof, and to sit under his shadow with great delight. These things are a remnant come unto, and do enjoy. This is the crown and rejoicing of the messengers and ministers of the Lord, when they come among us; to find us feeding on the bread of life; enjoying and possessing substance, peace, life and everlasting salvation: and it is their sorrow and trouble to find a people under the profession of truth, always learning, but never educated; always hearing, and yet ignorant of the voice of the word of life in themselves, and of that living bread which comes down from heaven.

LVIII. To them that believe, Christ is *precious*, specifically him whom the nations despise, and the master builders set at naught: I say, to those that believe he is precious, he is become the head of the corner. They love him in all his appearances, manifestations, dispensations and operations; whether he appear as a judge, a convincer, a reprover, a refiner with fire, and a fuller with soap; or a comforter, Savior, or prince of peace. In all these he is precious to those that believe in him, because they know and believe, that the blessed end of every appearance and operation of his Spirit in them, is in order to make them happy.

It is very blessed to know him appear as a judge, a reprover, a refiner and fuller, et cetera. This is more than a bare profession, and beyond all the nominal *Christians* upon the face of the earth; but it is much more blessed to know him a finisher of the work, to know judgment brought forth to victory, to know a being refined, a being purified, a being sanctified and saved. This is a state that every believer is to wait for and experience; without which, they cannot be *Christians* indeed, *Israelites* indeed, in who is no guile.

For this I testify, that this is the end of the blessed appearance of the Son of God, the *light, grace, Spirit, Power* or *love* of God *within*, which is all one thing, though under different names, so to work and operate in every true believer in him, and lover of him, as to make an end of sin, finish transgression, and bring in everlasting righteousness. This is the blessed end of all his operations.

The titular *Christian* that talks of Christ and his offices, as king, priest, and prophet, Savior and redeemer, et cetera, and knows him not first as a refiner, a fuller, a purger of the floor, and a burner of the chaff with unquenchable fire, deceives his own soul with a vain talk and profession; so never witnesses sin made an end of, nor transgression finished, nor everlasting righteousness brought in. Unless this be known, all profession is vain, and people cheat themselves with the name *Christian*, the nature thereof being lacking.

It is very precious and absolutely needful, for every individual that professes the name of Christ, and says that he is a believer in him, to feel and know his heart and mind truly in love with every appearance of him in his soul; to follow it and obey it, and to enjoy the end thereof, *that is to say*, everlasting salvation brought in, sin made an end of, that he may appear the second time without sin unto salvation. This is worthy to be waited for; and as every one loves the appearance of Christ, and joins to it in their hearts, against every appearance of evil, they are in the way that leads thereto, specifically to everlasting life, peace, and salvation. This is the new and living way, and there is not another. All that are out of this way, strangers to it in their minds, their hearts being alienated from it, never come to inherit substance, nor to know everlasting righteousness brought in, unrighteousness finished and cast forth, the house swept, purged, and cleansed, and they made an habitation for God in the spirit, but do remain as an cage for unclean birds, and a place for dragons; though they may talk of the fame of wisdom, sanctification and redemption, righteousness, and salvation, yet they are found in the contrary; in captivity and bondage, though they talk of freedom and redemption; in unholiness and corruption, while they talk of sanctification and righteousness. *Let all concerned, consider hereof.*

LIX. It is a blessed thing for people to meet together in one place *with one accord, all minding one thing*, every *mind exercised in the Spirit and in the Truth*, wherein alone God is worshipped. This is the worship that a remnant are brought unto, which worship does not always begin when their solemn meetings begin, neither does it end when they part. It is as every one is found therein, that they and their worship differ from all the formal worshippers upon the face of the whole earth, whose worship stands in the traditions and inventions of men, in set times, and at certain places, in saying certain prayers, reading diverse lessons, preaching and singing, et cetera. Every mind being exercised in the truth, every thing that is contrary thereunto, is made to bow and bend unto it; every thought, every imagination, every desire and affection made subject to the truth, worshipping or bowing to the name of Jesus. This is more than bowing the knee, or all bodily exercise whatsoever; more than all *mountain* and *Jerusalem* worship, of all the diverse modes in *Christendom*. For while the *mind* is carnally exercised, the *heart* corrupt, the *conscience* defiled, the *understanding* darkened; all is but will-worship, self-work, and voluntary humility, and has no acceptance with God.

LX. It is a true saying which Christ spoke to his Disciples, when he said, *If I go not away, the Comforter will not come.* There is much in the words; many have read them, but have not understood what they read; for it is a blessed thing to know the going away of Christ after the flesh, and to be able to say, as one of old did, *know I him so no more.* They are those that know him come again in the Spirit as a comforter, as a prince of peace, and are witnesses of his peaceable government in their souls, and can say, *he is come, and we look not for another.*

LXI. Of a truth, the times of *refreshing* are come from the presence of the Lord, the *showers* from Heaven are falling and *the heavenly Manna* is rained down, and many are livingly refreshed therewith, and are become as a well watered garden who were as a desert and wilderness, are now blossoming as a rose; and those that were barren, now bear and bring forth fruit unto God. This is the Lord's doing, and is marvelous in the eyes of a remnant.

Blessed are the people that can meet together with one accord, and sit before the Lord waiting upon him. Such at times are favored to sit as at a banquet, and have a table richly spread before them; they eat and drink and their souls are satisfied. Their everlasting happiness and blessedness stands in this; in feeling their hearts and minds continually drawn near unto the Lord, and staid upon him, not only in their solemn meetings, but at other times. In this they are preserved in a capacity to partake of the mercies and blessings of the Lord daily. This is a blessed and safe state indeed; to know a stay to the mind, to know the heart fixed, joined, settled upon the Lord. Such cannot be easily moved, neither can the enemy prevail against such, nor the stranger intermeddle with their joy. Their bread is sure, and their water fails not. They are witnesses of the truth of that prophet's words, who said, speaking of the Lord, *You will keep them in perfect peace, whose minds are staid upon you.* What can any desire more than perfect Peace? Peace that is entire, lacking nothing, full of satisfaction, and rejoicing in the inward man. Oh! what would a remnant have given in times past, to have known a stay to their minds, to have known the heavenly treasure, which is sufficient to satisfy, refresh and console their souls! This is the pearl of great price. This is the eating of the tree of life indeed, and is the only way and means to come to the possession of all the treasures of wisdom and knowledge that lie hid in Christ Jesus, and to inherit all the blessings that attend the *Christian* religion we profess; but those that are of a wandering mind, their thoughts, wills and affections unsubdued, unmortified, they are in that state wherein they know not when good comes, and as broken cisterns that can hold no water.

Meditations & Experiences

So this is the main thing, wherein our safety and happiness stands, *namely*, to know our minds and hearts drawn near unto the Lord, our eye fixed upon him; that after we have partook of his blessings, and been refreshed with his presence, we may abide in a frame of mind, ready to receive of him that which does satisfy our souls, and minister true content to our minds. Nothing is able thus to do, but the daily bread. What we eat to day, will not serve to-morrow. *Give us this day our daily bread.* Bread every day fresh from the table of the Lord. Hereby is the growing from grace to grace, from faith to faith, from one degree of glory unto another witnessed, specifically till we all come unto the stature and fullness of Christ. The more any thus truly wait to enjoy, the more they feel their strength renewed with heavenly encouragement, so that they can *run and not be weary*, and *walk and not be faint*.

LXII. That which makes a people blessed and happy, is, *that they hear and obey* the still small voice, which says, *this is the way, walk in it*. This is the voice of the true shepherd, and the sheep know it, follow it and obey it, and a stranger they will not hear nor follow. In this lay the safety, strength and blessedness of the righteous, in all ages and generations past, specifically in hearing and obeying the voice of the Lord. Herein they gained victory over their enemies, and knew them all confounded and brought to naught. This is the strength and blessedness of the righteous in this age and generation, by which they overcome their enemies. As we hear and obey this voice, we grow strong and prevail against all our enemies, specifically those of our own house, which are our greatest enemies. In obeying this heavenly voice, which calls out of all the crooked ways and bye-paths of sin and transgression, into the straight and living way of the Lord, and preserves in the same, that we return not into them again, that we enter not into the way of sin and transgression, that we are not captivated in the way of darkness and error, out of which we have been called, and from which we have been redeemed and saved with a great salvation. Praises be to the name of the Lord, who has caused his glorious day to dawn, and his heavenly voice to be heard and known, from all the voices that are in the world, and from the voice of the serpent, though it many times speaks very low and small. Yet blessed be the Lord, we hear and know it from the voice of our enemy, from the voice of the stranger, because it calls out of all evil and error, into purity and holiness; out of all self-will, thoughts and imaginations, into the heavenly stillness, self-denial, deep humility, and lowliness of mind; which is the low valley where the fresh pastures are, and the springs of life are known where satisfaction is enjoyed, and peace and tranquility of mind possessed. This is the substance of all. This is that we have been and are called to, in this the glorious day of God's appearance, in this his visitation of us with his day-spring from on high, which shines gloriously to a remnant; praises to God for ever.

LXIII. Those are the blessed people, *who have not their teacher to seek, their Savior and redeemer to seek*; but their eye *beholds him*, and their ear *hears his voice*; witnessing and enjoying what one of old knew, when he said, *I know that my redeemer lives, and that he shall stand last upon the earth.* This is a heavenly state, which a small remnant witnesses, specifically to see their redeemer *stand last upon the earth.* He was the first upon it, and is known to be the last also; subduing all under him; the earth to be his footstool; all earthly-mindedness, earthly desires, earthly affections, trodden down and trampled upon by him; every vain thought and lofty imagination subdued under him, all our enemies destroyed by him. But no people nor person upon the face of the earth, can witness these things effected in them, but as they travail through the work of Regeneration, and come to know that their Redeemer lives, not only in himself, but also in them. Then transgression is known to be finished, and everlasting righteousness brought in. Then the prince of peace and righteousness reigns, sits upon the throne and rules; where the prince of the power of the air and unrighteousness did rule. Then does the land rejoice, and heavenly peace abounds in their dwellings; which peace cannot be enjoyed by any, let them profess what they will, though it be the truth itself, unless they experimentally know their teacher, their Savior, their redeemer.

LXIV. The very remembrance of the time, wherein our minds were turned *to the true light that now shines*, not only in darkness, but out of it, is very precious; in which God *dwells*, in which we are living witnesses of his *presence* and *appearance*; which ministers more consolation, refreshment and gladness in our hearts, than the increase of corn, wine and oil. The exceeding love and kindness of God, in fitting and preparing instruments in his own hand, and by his own power, to turn and direct our minds to the light of Christ within, to the Power of God within, is never to be forgotten. The waiting in which, and the obedience to which, makes us and our assemblies to differ from those who are strangers thereunto; the which, as we wait in and obey, we never have our teacher to seek, our guide and instructor to seek, though no word be spoken outwardly.

It is a precious thing to love this light, and to walk in it. That is the only way to be a child of it. It is the high way that was prophesied should *be cast up, wherein the wayfaring man, though a fool, should not err.* There is no stumbling in this way, nor *no occasion of stumbling.* As we walk and abide therein, we are, and shall be the most contented people, the wisest, strongest and happiest people upon the face of the Earth; but out of it, we are as weak as any: and after we are come to the knowledge of this way, if we abide not herein, we may also become as wicked as any.

There is no other way to be looked for, no other Gospel to be preached than this, to which our minds were turned at the beginning, *that is to say,* the *light,* the *grace, and Power of God,* the *pearl,* the *treasure,* the *kingdom within;* in which the key is known, that opens not only the mysteries of Godliness, but the mystery of iniquity also; and brings our eye to be satisfied with seeing, our ear with hearing, and our heart with understanding.

Oh! how are we engaged to walk in this way! to walk worthy of this love which is shed abroad in our hearts, which we are made partakers of, that we may adorn our profession with all holiness of life and conversation, to the praise of Him, that has called us out of darkness into his marvelous light: to whom the glory for ever.

LXV. It is a blessed thing, to know *the Kingdom of God to be come,* specifically the same kingdom which Christ long since taught his Disciples to pray for; and which he, in this age, has taught his Disciples to pray for. It is a blessed thing to know this kingdom to be come, but it is more blessed to know a sitting down in it, and partaking of that wherein it stands, *namely, peace and joy in the Holy Ghost*; which all the kingdoms of this world cannot give nor take away.

Now the cause why we in time past, as well as others, were ignorant of the coming of this kingdom, and lacked the enjoyment of that wherein it stands, was because we disregarded its appearance, and overlooked the seed of it, and slighted the operation of it; which is like the working of leaven in meal. This was the cause, specifically because we did not regard the day of small things; we had no faith in the holy Power and spiritual appearance of God within, which always wrought against evil, and the author of it, and his kingdom of darkness, though but as a little leaven, or small seed.

And all the sects and sect-masters in *Christendom*, who overlook the seed of the kingdom, which works like leaven in all that have faith in it, and despise the appearance and operation of the light and Spirit of God within, they never know the coming of the kingdom of God, nor the sitting down in it. They inherit vanity, reap sorrow, and lie down in misery, let their talk and profession be never so high. *This is the word of Truth to them all.*

But all that know the coming of this kingdom, and a sitting down in it, and the enjoyment of that wherein it stands, which is peace and joy in the Holy Ghost; they are living witnesses of their being gathered from the east, west, north and south, and of sitting down with *Abraham, Isaac, and Jacob,* in the kingdom of God, and can say as some of old could, which the author to the *Hebrews* wrote to when he said, *But you are come unto Mount* Zion, *and unto the city of the living God; the heavenly* Jerusalem, *and to an innumerable company of angels, to the general assembly and church of the first-born, which are written in Heaven; and to God the judge of all, and to the spirits of just men made perfect; and to Jesus, the Mediator of the new covenant; and to the blood of sprinkling, that speaks better things than the blood of* Abel. Were not these things written in the Holy Scriptures, it might or would be counted unlawful, if not blasphemy, to speak or write after this manner. But the kingdom and Power of God is one and the same throughout all ages, and was the dwelling place of the righteous in all generations; specifically the same our minds were at first turned and directed to, whose first appearance was as a *light* shining in a dark place; as a *little seed* springing out of a dry ground; as a *little leaven* working in the meal, according to the parables and teachings of Christ Jesus. This was the lot and inheritance, which the holy men and holy women in ages past waited for and received, and glorified and praised God for the enjoyment thereof, in the midst of all afflictions and fiery trials, and over them all. This was their joy and crown, and the righteous in this age desire no other.

LXVI. We have been and are called to *inherit substance*; and all that have obeyed this call, and abode with him that has called, are witnesses of *that bread which nourishes up unto eternal life!* and do experience the preciousness and pleasantness that there is, *in eating of that bread which comes down from Heaven.* The outward bread, upon the outward Table, in the outward temple, was a type and representation of this heavenly bread, which nourishes those that feed thereon up unto eternal life. To meet together, and sit together at this table, and eat of this bread, is better than to sit on thrones with princes, and to eat of their delicacies. All the treasures and pleasures of this world are not to be compared with it; for there is nothing able to content the soul, and to stop its hungering and thirsting after those things that perish with the using, but the eating of this bread: and the more any eat of this bread, the more they hunger after it. There is a pleasure and blessing in hungering and thirsting, when the treasury of living bread and water is ready at hand to supply; and it is the taste of the crumbs which fall from the children's table, that begets a cry in the hearts of a remnant: *Evermore give us this bread*.

LXVII. Blessed are all who have their eye unto the Lord, and their ear open unto him at all times, and in all places, and in all states and conditions; for of a truth, *God is come to teach his people himself*, as was long since foretold. All that have learned of him, and are guided by his Spirit, are thereby led to within the veil into the holiest of holies, and know the veil to be taken away, not only the veil of *Moses*, and the veil of the outward *temple*; but, also, the veil of *the flesh of Christ*; and are come to behold him, and dwell with him, who was before the cause of veils had a being; before the cause of the law, the labor of the prophets, and suffering of Christ had a being. This state is precious to behold, and very delightful to enjoy. This is the light of his countenance indeed, which *is better than corn, wine, oil, or all visible things*.

This is the blessed end of waiting upon God, as the handmaid does upon the eye of her mistress. Whether you are as a babe, as a child, as a young man, as an elder, or as a father; your duty is in all these states and growths, to have your eye unto the Lord, that he may lead you from the one into the other, and preserve you therein by his grace, which is able and sufficient to teach you all good, save and defend you from all evil, lead you into glory, and establish you in the kingdom thereof for ever.

LXVIII. It is a very blessed thing, and those are the people that are come to a blessed state and condition, who can say in truth, that *their bodies are the temples of the Holy Ghost*. These are they whose eyes behold their teacher; their eye is inward unto him, who teaches in his temple, and whose glory appears in his temple. These are the blessed people that have this knowledge; and all that have it, know how they come by it, and how they became so, having been the temples of the unclean spirit. They know the temple that was defiled and polluted, cleansed and purged, and the unclean spirit and his works cast forth. These are a watchful people against all that would defile the temple again, and these are the true temple worshippers in this day and age, and this is the temple in which every one speaks of the *Glory of the Lord*, of the *Power of the Lord*, and of his *wondrous works wrought therein, even in his temple not made with hands.*

This is the antitype and substance of the outward temple built by *Solomon*, and the various worships and services therein; specifically when people are brought into such a state, as to know their bodies the temple of the living God; that he walks in them, and dwells in them, according to the ancient prophecies of holy men. These are a habitation of God through the Spirit.

These are the worshippers in *Spirit*, in *Truth*, not only in appointed places and solemn assemblies, but at other times and places, bowing to every appearance of God in his temple, in the Spirit and in the Truth in the inward parts, which God loves, accepts and delights in.

The outward temple, after it was finished and sanctified, became defiled, polluted, and made as a den of thieves; therefore it became robbed and spoiled of all its treasure, and so in the end destroyed. This was, or came to pass in the figure, and is written for our learning; *Let all be watchful and take heed, lest after they know their bodies the temples of God, sanctified or made holy, they become polluted and defiled again.* Such God will destroy with woeful destruction.

It is very precious when people are come not only to know their bodies the temples of the Holy Ghost, which knowledge is absolutely needful, for without it there is no being a *Christian*, but also are come to know an heavenly stillness, an heavenly silence in the temple, no buying and selling, nor exchanging; no noise of the workman's iron tool in the temple, for that defiles the temple, and pollutes the altar, if it be but lifted up upon it. The best parts, inventions and arts of man in the fall, has nothing to do in rearing an altar, in building a temple, nor in setting up a worship, or offering sacrifices to God. His righteousness and his wickedness are both abomination to the Lord.

LXIX. The Gospel is *the Power of God unto salvation*. This Gospel was preached in *Abraham's* time, yes in *Enoch's* and *Adam's* time, and salvation was obtained in it and by it. Those that obeyed this Gospel, the Power of God, in those ages, were saved by it *from evil, made just and holy men, friends of God, and walked with him.* Thus it was before the law, under the law, through the prophets. All that obeyed the Spirit and Power of God, obeyed the Gospel, and were redeemed and saved by it *from sin and transgression*, which mankind being fallen into, had need of the Gospel to be preached unto him; had need of redemption and salvation by it; and as it is received and obeyed, it is known to be the Power of God to salvation by such.

Paul's testimony was, *Col.* I. 23 that he was a *minister of that Gospel which was preached in every creature under heaven*; which was indeed the universal *light, love* and *Power of God*, appearing for the salvation of man. All that are true ministers of this Gospel, are like their heavenly Father, whose light shines for all, whose rain falls upon all, whose love extends to all. They are not like the *Jewish* Rabbis, Doctors and priests, or ministers of the *letter*; who preach not *the Power of God*, that brings salvation to all that receive and obey it; neither do they bring their *disciples into true love, peace, unity, good-will and brotherly-kindness one to another, and to all mankind, and put an end to the contrary.*

Oh! the miserable state poor mankind is brought into, and held captive in, through the mystery of iniquity working in many of the nominal professors in nominal *Christendom* where under the name and profession of the prince of peace, love, goodwill, innocence, patience, kindness, and all holy virtues, is really found and practiced, wars, fighting, cruelty, violence, envying, hating and destroying one another; which are not the fruits of the Gospel of God, nor of the ministry thereof; but *of men, of the prince of confusion*, and *of* Babylon, and of those who have drunk of the whore's cup, whose wine of fornication, has made drunk all nations. *He that can understand, let him.*

LXX. Blessed are all those that *know themselves members of the true Church*, which is built of living stones, elect and precious, and are made an habitation for God, in the Spirit, and in the Truth, who meet together, and wait upon the Lord in silence, and worship in Spirit and Truth, without a book, or dependence on a man-minister.

So blessed are all that are of the true Church, living stones, a spiritual house, and habitation for God, who know him to dwell in them, and to walk in them as in his temple, teaching and ruling in their hearts. These are fellow-citizens with the Saints in Light, and know the heavenly city, *Jerusalem*, come down from Heaven, and themselves, inhabitants thereof. These have known Redemption from the earth, and the tongue of the *Egyptian* sea dried up, the seat of the whore, and the mystery of all her harlotry, under all her various dresses and sumptuous array, and golden appearances discovered; and these are they that cannot be deceived longer by them. These can sing *Hallelujah*, Salvation, and Glory, and Honor, and Power unto the Lord their God. These can say, *true and righteous are his judgments*, for he has judged the great whore, which did corrupt the earth with her fornication, and has avenged the blood of his servants at her hand. These can say, *Praise our God, all you his servants, and you that fear him, both small and great, for the Lord God Omnipotent reigns; let us be glad and rejoice, and give honor to him, for the marriage of the Lamb is come, and his wife has made herself ready, being arrayed in fine linen, clean and white, which is the righteousness of Saints, and is the wedding garment that all are to be clothed with, who are called to the marriage supper of the Lamb, who are members of his body, which is his Church.*

A
TREATISE
CONCERNING
THOUGHTS & IMAGINATIONS.

Evil thoughts and imaginations are great troubles of the world; and it is a great misery which man is accompanied and surrounded with, who is given up to follow and obey his own evil thoughts and imaginations; or to walk according to them: it was a harsh judgment pronounced against the disobedient rebellious Jews, in the word of the Lord by *Jeremiah*, saying, *Hear, O Earth, behold I will bring evil upon this people, even the fruit of their thoughts.* And the Lord by the prophet *Isaiah*, said, *I have stretched out my hand all day to a rebellious people, which walked in a way that was not good, after their own thoughts, which are thoughts of iniquity, and the act of violence is in their hands.* Also, it is written, *every thought and imagination of man's heart is only evil, and that continually.* And very great is the misery bondage, and slavery of mankind in this estate; he is an enemy to God, and to himself, and to his neighbor and brother; *wasting and destruction are in their paths, who have not God in all their thoughts.*

Now, reader, that which is principally on my mind, is, to set before you a certain infallible way, how you may come to be saved from following or obeying your own thoughts, and to gain strength against, and get victory over all your imaginations that are evil; and, also, how you may attain to good thoughts and heavenly meditations in the room thereof; and how you may come to know every good thought and desire brought into the obedience of Christ, and every evil thought and imagination destroyed and consumed with the breath of his mouth; and the brightness of his appearing. And when you are restored and brought into the same estate man was in before transgression, even into the garden of God, how you must then dress and keep the garden. You must then watch over, and in the wisdom and Power of God, govern your thoughts, lest the serpent beguile you as he did *Eve*.

First. You must understand that from the ground, evil thoughts and imaginations arise from, spring all the briers, thorns and thistles, and other hurtful weeds in the world of mankind, in whose heart they began to spring, grow and increase, even so soon as he began to lose his faith in God his Maker, and incline to hearken to the voice of the serpent, and give credit to his lies, which begot a vain thought; from whence a false hope sprung, that they should, by eating the forbidden fruit, better their conditions, *be as Gods*, according as the serpent told the woman, the weaker vessel, and by this false hope, grounded upon the thoughts and imaginations, entered the first transgression; then when the temptation was entered into, and sin committed, thoughts and imaginations began to multiply and fill the disobedient earthly heart of man, who, having now turned his back upon the heavenly, slighted the voice and command of God, who was his *teacher* and *lawgiver*, and lent his ear to the wicked one, and gave up his mind and heart to obey him, even with thoughts it was all for the best. Thus poor man being deceived with vain thoughts, and false hope, lost his habitation and dwelling-place in paradise; which after he had transgressed, he still thought to keep: for he was soon convinced he had done amiss in eating the forbidden fruit; and fear possess his heart, when he heard the voice of God in the cool of the day, and therefore sought means to cover and hide himself from the sight of God: but herein his thoughts were vain, and his endeavors to no purpose; the woman, man, and serpent, all received the fruits of their own doings; nothing but life, good and blessing were known before; now death, evil and cursing, the fruit and effect of disobedience, (which as I have said, entered first by giving place a vain thought and desire, in hope to gain and better their estate,) became the daily companions of mankind, who found and still find by woeful experience, that saying true, *when sin is finished it brings forth death*.

So man having lost his place in the garden which God planted, through neglecting his work which God appointed him to do, which *was to dress it, and to keep it*; (for the garden needed dressing and keeping before the forbidden fruit was eaten;) innocence was lost, and sin was committed.

And this arises in my mind to testify to all the wise in heart; that after they come to find that which was lost, to witness a restoration and regeneration, and a returning into *Eden*, into innocence, they have work there to do; *dressing* and *keeping* are two very significant words; this was the business of man in the beginning, in the state of innocence; if he had not neglected this work, slighted the light, power, wisdom and glory of God with which he was replenished, he had never fallen; when the temptation got into a thought, if he had watched in the light and wisdom of God, he would have seen and discovered the tendency of it, and have prevented its coming to a desire and act: but first giving place to a selfish thought, it soon sprang to a hunger or desire, thence into act; this is the beginning and progress of sin at this day, which mankind, in innocence, had, and still has power and wisdom from God to prevent, if he abide in it, and keep in his watchtower, the light and strength of God, which is as near him as the temptation can be, and sufficient to preserve him: and where this work is neglected, men, yes, holy men fall, and sin after the similitude of *Adam's* transgression, and are beguiled as the serpent did *Eve*, drawn out of innocence, and a sinless estate after they have attained unto it; therefore let none be high-minded, but fear and take the second *Adam* for example, who when he was tempted, did not desire after the things presented, though very specious in appearance, and accompanied with very large promises; even as the first *Adam* had; but it is written, while the temptation lasted he ate nothing; he let nothing in, gave no place to selfish thoughts, and enticements of the enemy: So when the temptation was over, angels ministered unto him: let this be the example of all the children of the light, and as they do thereafter, the powerful salvation of God shall surround them, *and neither heights nor depths, angels, principalities, nor powers, things present, or things to come shall be able to separate them from the love of God in Christ Jesus.* This is as a word by the way.

Now evil thoughts and imaginations are of a multiplying nature, and do mainly increase and take root in the generality of mankind, who through evil works are estranged from the life of God, remaining a degenerate plant, sprung from the seed of the evil doer, and dwells and labors in that ground which God has cursed, and knows not the seed of the woman to bruise the serpent's head, and to redeem and preserve him from following and obeying his own thoughts and imaginations which are evil, and that continually. And indeed in that state can be no otherwise, whether they lead into self-sinning or self-righteousness, both are abominations to the Lord, and destructive to the well-being of mankind, both temporal and eternal: for all the wickedness that has been brought forth and acted in the world since the beginning, began or appeared first in the thought; and the thought being cherished and joined to by the mind, will, and understanding, it increased, and increases into words and actions. That which is clean cannot proceed from that which is unclean; the heart of mankind in the fall is universally corrupted, and desperately wicked: and, as has been said, the thoughts and imaginations thereof are evil, and that continually: and before it can be otherwise, there is an absolute necessity that every individual man and woman know and experience for, and in themselves, their hearts cleansed, purged and purified and created anew; the ground must be made good, before the seed, the heavenly plant can grow, increase and flourish therein; before good thoughts, heavenly thoughts and meditations can arise, spring and remain therein. And when this estate is known and enjoyed, then to abide with him dwell and walk with him, who has wrought these mighty things in you, and for you, and in his wisdom and power to dress and keep the garden, the heart, with all diligence, that that which would defile enter not, creep not in again, as it did in the beginning, which is possible. Therefore what the Spirit of God put man upon in the beginning, when he was a noble plant in *Eden*, wholly a right seed, *namely*, to dress and keep the garden; so the Spirit of God now in this age said, *watch and pray, lest you enter into temptation; take heed, lest as the serpent beguiled* Eve, *through his subtlety, so your minds should be corrupted from the simplicity that is in Christ.*

Now this I testify from certain knowledge, that God has ordained means, whereby mankind, whose heart is so corrupted, that nothing that is good proceeds out of it, neither any thing that is heavenly, and of God, springs up in it, that can live a moment, being so foul and so dark, even like a foul dark piece of earth outwardly on which the sun never shines, nor the rain falls, that man in this miserable state may come to know and experience his foul heart cleansed, purged, and sanctified, as the Christians in the primitive times did; *such were some of you, but now are you washed, cleansed, and sanctified,* et cetera, *the fallow ground may be ploughed up, and bear seed, and the wilderness may become a fruitful field, and streams may break forth in the desert, and the desert may come to rejoice and to blossom as a rose; crooked things may be made strait, and rough places smooth; great heavy dark high mountains may be brought down and removed, yes melted at the presence of God, and the low valleys may be exalted; yes the wilderness may become like* Eden, *and the desert like the garden of the Lord.* All these mighty works and wonders has the Lord wrought in this age, in and for a remnant, who are come to the fulfilling of the prophecies, are living witnesses of the same, and do in his Holy Spirit and Power, proclaim that the love and mercy of God towards man is universal, and that his hand is stretched forth to help him out of the snare, pit, and deep dark dungeon, wherein he is fallen; out of which he cannot by all his strength,

Thoughts & Imaginations

wisdom, and invention, help himself; and to set him at liberty, that he may run the ways of his commandments with delight, and that he may come again to stand upright, as God made man in the beginning; and lay aside all his thoughts and inventions, wherein he corrupted himself; and to bring him into such a state and condition, that he may be able to do all things that are good, to think Good thoughts, speak good words, and do good works; and so eschew and avoid the contrary: this to know and be able to do, is the *one thing* needful, without which all men are miserable, let their knowledge, wisdom, and profession of religion, opinion and invention, be what it will.

Therefore my desire is, in good-will to mankind, having received knowledge and understanding of the means God has ordained for their good and salvation: and being something acquainted with the two great mysteries of godliness and iniquity, and the way and working of each, to impart and signify something of the same in a few words, to instruct and inform those to whom this my testimony may come, how they may attain thereunto, and how they may come to be rid of those troublesome companions, *that is to say*, evil thoughts and imaginations, that arise in their hearts, while corrupted; and how the same may be purified and made a holy habitation for God, as it was before sin entered, before innocence was lost, before the serpent deceived the weaker vessel, when all was good, yes, very good.

The way that leads thereto, I declare to be as follows; and whoever you are that has a mind or desire to find that which is lost, observe, believe, and receive what I say or write, as *truth*; not received or learned by tradition, but by the experimental powerful work and operation of the Spirit of truth in your own mind; and what I have said, or shall say, is, and shall be according to the holy scriptures, and witnessed to by them for I cannot write contrary to them, being in unity with them, and with the just men's spirits that wrote them. First then know you, O Man! whoever you are, and whatever your thoughts and imaginations are, how far so ever you are run into corruption, darkness, and degeneration from the state of innocence, purity, and holiness; yet there is a measure of divine light attends you; though you are darkness, it shines in you, in order to show you your way out of it; though you are degenerated and run from God into the earth, yet this pure light and Spirit of God follows you, and calls you back; and you may in this state hear it as a voice behind you, saying *return, return, this is the way, come and walk in it*; this is the kindness and love of God to you in his Son;

who is the light of the world, and enlightens every one that comes there into; if you hear and obey this voice of the light of the Son of God, though you were dead in sin, and buried as in a grave, you shall arise and come forth and live before him; the bars and gates of Hell shall not be able to retain you: but if you slight and despise the light of God that visits you and shuts your ear against its voice, it will be as a thousand witnesses against you, while you rebels against it, and are found following your own thoughts and imaginations, and doing the thing that is evil; for this light I speak of, is the eye of the Lord, that runs to and fro through the earth, beholding the evil and the good, and that discerns the thoughts and intents of the heart; it is the word that is near in the mouth and in the heart, which is quick and powerful, sharper than any two-edged sword, piercing specifically to the dividing asunder of soul and spirit, and of the joints and marrow: this is the candle of the Lord that searches *Jerusalem*, and gives light to the sides of the earth, and corners of the world from whom the *shadow of death* cannot hide, nor the *rocks and mountains* cover or defend; *for he that forms the mountains, and creates the winds, and declares or shows unto man what is his thought, that makes the morning darkness, and treads upon the high places of the earth, the Lord, the God of Hosts is his name.* This is the Spirit of truth that convinces the world of sin, and that sets men's sins in order before them, and reproves and smites in secret for evil, and that brings to judgment the hidden things of *Esau*: from this eye or light of the Lord, you canst not hide yourself no more than *Adam* and *Cain* could, though you should hate the light, which shows you your thoughts, and love the darkness so as to dwell in it, yet the light or eye of God will pursue you and find you out; Hell, nor the utmost parts of the earth, and darkness, cannot secure you from the just condemnation of God; because you hates the shining of his light, and stop your ear against the voice and teaching of it, and love the darkness and dwell in it, while you does so, you chooses the way of death, and neglects the means of salvation that God has ordained: for this is the *condemnation of the world, that light is come into it, and men love darkness rather, because their deeds are evil.*

Now at the first step towards restoration and everlasting happiness, you are required to turn your mind from the darkness in which you dwell, to the light, eye or Spirit of God, and to decline the power of Satan that works in the darkness, and embrace the Power of God; and when you doest but begin to do so, you wilt find the scales to fall from your eyes by degrees, and the veil to be taken off your heart, and the fetters and chains of darkness to be loosed, and the prison doors opened; so when your candle is lighted, and your eye opened, you wilt discern your way out, and see the angel of the Lord go before you, and guide you in the same: and you wilt also perceive what is in your house, and clearly understand what has lodged in the dark room of your heart, and when you comes to see things as they are (Mistake in the understanding concerning the nature of things that do present themselves before mankind is the cause of error. Thence it is that some call darkness light, and light darkness), you wilt receive wisdom to give them names according to their nature, and to judge righteously concerning them: and as you love this light, you wilt be enabled by it to divide between thought and thought, and begin to make conscience of a thought; and to hate every vain thought, and when you cannot be easily rid of them, nor remove them from their old lodging-place, you wilt breathe and cry to the Lord in the spirit, as one of old did, who was burdened and oppressed with their company; *Search me and try me, O God! and know my heart, try me, and know my thoughts, and see if there be any wicked way in me, and lead me in the way everlasting.* This is the cry which the Lord hears, and will answer in due and needful time. And *Jeremiah's* cry to *Jerusalem* was, *wash your heart from wickedness, that you may be saved, how long shall your vain thoughts lodge within you?* Now the only way to dislodge them, and to be rid of their company, is to show them no countenance, make no provision for them, give them no entertainment, but by the light of God, which discovers them to be your enemies, judge them, and keep your mind exercised in the light and Power of God, that it is turned to; and in your thoughts and imaginations, give them no regard: and though they do and may arise, pursue and compass you about like bees, yet you, keeping your eye fixed in the light and Power of God, which is as near you as your thoughts are, and shows them unto you, you wilt see them in due time scattered as chaff before a fierce wind, and destroyed as stubble before a devouring fire.

Now as you come to be a believer in the light, and to trust in the Power of God, to which your mind is turned, you wilt become in very deed a child of it, and soon be able to say, darkness is past, and the true light now shines, by which you can see and judge every thought and motion that arises and stirs in your mind, whether evil or innocent, hurtful or harmless, and have wisdom to order them accordingly. And this is that primitive wisdom man had in the beginning, but he abode not in it, through looking at the temptation and beauty of the thing presented to the eye of his mind. The woman was deceived in her thoughts; in her judgment and understanding was she beguiled before she obeyed the tempter; it appeared *good for food, pleasant and desirable*, and able to make one wise, before she ate, or gave to her husband[1]. *Paul* said, the woman being deceived, was in the transgression subjected to vanity; not willingly, but through hope[2]; she hoped to find the serpent's words true; and to become more wise, and more happy, by taking the serpent's counsel[3]; but instead thereof, fell into the depth of misery: the same danger attends the children of light; the sons and daughters of God; for *Adam* was a son of God before transgression; and it is only such who are in the restoration, children of the light, and of the day, that are capable to fall as *Adam* and *Eve* did, and to sin after the similitude of *Adam's* transgression, and to lose innocence, purity, holiness and uprightness as they did, and be driven out of the garden of God, as they were. Such as were never in it, nor ever dwelt in the state of restoration, innocence, purity, and holiness, cannot be said to fall from, or lost it. Children of darkness, and children of the devil, who have gone astray, and dwelt in darkness, and in the region and shadow of death, never knew what the life of purity and holiness is, nor what the simplicity of the gospel of Christ is, so cannot be beguiled as the serpent did *Eve*, of that they never knew, nor had, as men and women now in the world; yet such are beguiled by the serpent in another sort; not of what they have had, and did once enjoy, but of what they might have, and should enjoy; and this he effects by keeping the eyes and minds of people abroad, and by persuading them to follow any thing, and walk in any way, rather than to turn the eye of their minds inward to the *light, word, Power*, and *Spirit of God*, which *shines*, which *speaks*, which *works in man*, in order to *lead*, to *teach* to *guide* and *direct* him in the way of life, and salvation, and to bring him into the glorious liberty of the sons of God, into a perfect translation from darkness to light, and from the

---

[1] *Gen. iii. 6.*

[2] *1 Tim. iii. 14.*

[3] *Rom. viii. 20,*

kingdom and power of Satan, to the kingdom and Power of the Son of God, and to know Christ made unto him wisdom, sanctification, and redemption.

This is the blessed end of God in sending his Son a light into the world, specifically to enlighten the *Gentile, Jew*, professor and profane; and that through him they might believe and receive eternal life, and enter into that blessed rest that God has prepared, which the primitive *Christians* who believed, entered into; where they did not speak their own words, nor think their own thoughts, nor do their own works, *their heavenly father spoke in them, and their thoughts were thoughts of God, and he wrought all their works in them and for them*. This is a blessed state indeed; and none are entered into the rest, which God has prepared; but such as are come to witness and experience these things, now in this age, as the primitive *Christians* did in ages past.

For while any are found thinking their own thoughts, speaking their own words, and doing their own works, though under a profession of Christ and *Christianity*, they cannot enter into the rest which God has prepared, though they may create to themselves false rests, and kindle a fire, and walk by the light of their own sparks, but in the end lie down in sorrow.

True rest and peace is obtained, or comes through a true self-denial: a dying to self-sinning, and self-righteousness, self-thinking and working, contriving and inventing, self-wisdom and understanding also: all these things must be denied, annihilated or brought to nothing, and confounded. The feeding upon these things occasioned, and occasioned the curse, and all the labor, trouble, sorrow and torment that has attended, and does attend mankind since the fall; to the death must they all come before a sitting down in the kingdom of God can be witnessed, or before any can cease from their own works, as God did from his[4].

Now you who are a child of light, *understand* this one thing for your comfort and encouragement in your warfare against evil thoughts; that notwithstanding a multitude of thoughts do arise in you, and troops thereof attend you, which are in themselves sinful; yet if you join not with them in your mind, will, and understanding, they are not your thoughts, neither shall the evil thereof be imputed unto you, if you loves the light, and keeps your mind joined to the Spirit of God, or appearance of Christ in you, that discovers all temptations unto

---

[4] *The feeding on the forbidden fruit, which was good in itself, though not for food, occasioned, and occasions at this day, all the miseries that attend mankind.*

you, in the very thought and first appearance of them; and you are helping the Lord against the mighty; being joined unto him, are becoming one with him in your mind and Spirit, though in your members there is a *law*, a *power* that wars against you, and as you abides with the Lord, waiting upon him, even as *the eye of a maid waits upon the hand of her mistress*; he will save and deliver you, and subdue all your enemies, even those of your own house, which are the greatest enemies.

Though temptations may, and will attend you, yet it is no sin to be tempted, though with inward temptations; neither are you to account yourself, nor to be accounted a sinner, because sin and vain thoughts may present themselves in you, in your warfare estate, yet you may say as *Paul* did, *It is no more I, but sin that dwells in me; and, that in me, that is in my flesh, dwells no good thing*: which flesh, you are now in the way to know, withers as the grass, and the glory of it, becomes as the faded flower of the field, and sin that dwells therein destroyed, and the creature of God's making preserved, the earthen vessel that holds the heavenly treasure sanctified and saved, and delivered from the yoke of bondage the whole creation of God groans under. And this you shall certainly arrive at, as you keeps your eye upon your *Savior*, your *light*, your *way*, your *captain*, whom you wilt see go before you conquering, and to conquer, till all his and your enemies are subdued, brought under and destroyed, and you made as a king, as a priest to God[5], and as the primitive *Christians* were, who could say: *As he is, so are we in this present world, pure as he is pure, holy as he is holy, righteous as he is righteous*, harmless and innocent as he was, in all resigned up unto the will of God: not my will, said the second *Adam*, but *thine*; though his will was as innocent and harmless as the first *Adam's* was before the fall, and did excel. When you comes up hither, you wilt understand, and receive what I say, till then it will be as a mystery, and a hard saying unto you.

And in your way, take heed of thinking, willing, and running; that obtains not the prize; stand still and see the salvation of God; mind, above all, the arm of his Power in you, which is able to suppress your thoughts, mortify your will, stop your running, and give you perfect strength to resist the devil, and make him flee, and to furnish you to every good word and work, and, give you

---

[5] *Lest thou should stumble at those sayings, consider that John was the greatest prophet that was born of woman, yet the least in the kingdom was greater than he.*

dominion over your own spirit whose property is to be swift in thought; eager in desire, and restless in the accomplishment thereof.

Now it is written[6], he that has rule over *his own spirit is stronger than he that takes a city; and he that has no rule over his own spirit, is like a city broken down, and without walls: when the righteous bears rule, the land rejoices; but when the wicked, the land mourns.* These things are infallibly true; while the usurper keeps the throne, the Prince of Peace, and his peaceable government is not known. Tribulation and anguish comes upon every soul of man that does evil, that thinks and imagines evil, and that yields his members servants to unrighteousness, let his opinion, profession, and talk of religion, be what it will, *he that commits sin, is of the devil:* and without returning from it, a finishing or ending of it, and righteousness set up in the room thereof, will have the wages and reward of the same, and possess the fruit of their own thoughts and doings.

Now it is a heavenly estate to live under the government of Christ, to know and experience him, swaying the scepter in the heart, and established in the throne thereof: but this none come to enjoy, till they have first known him to sit as a refiner with fire, and as a fuller with soap; and as a spirit of judgment and burning; and as the stronger to dispossess the strongman, spoil all his goods, sweep and cleanse the house, and to furnish it again with heavenly goods, thoughts, desires, and meditations, and all things else that becomes the house of the Lord: holiness to the Lord was written or engraved upon the crown and plate of gold, and all the furniture of the outward temple was sanctified, of which this is the antitype, or substance, as he that enjoys it well knows.

And now it is the duty of a *Christian* to watch in the light against evil thoughts, and to use the axe of God, which is laid to the root of them, that their springing again may be hindered, and the end of them prevented; so also it is the duty of every one, when good thoughts and desires spring in the room thereof, to cherish them, to join with them, and to keep their eye unto the Lord that begat them, or raised them up in the heart; being thoughts of purity, thoughts of peace and righteousness, thoughts of holiness and joy in the inward man; which thoughts you of yourself cannot think: these are comfortable thoughts, justifying and excusing thoughts, thoughts that will stand approved in the light, and the

---

[6] *Consider the simile, and in the light, try and compare yourself therewith, and thou wilt find the truth thereof.*

end and tendency of them is good, even as pleasant fruit to the soul; so that such can say as *David* once did: *How precious are your thoughts unto me, O God! how great is the sum of them if I should count them, they are more in number than the sand; when I awake I am still with you*[7]. As you loves the light, and delights in the law of God, and meditates therein[8], these good thoughts will multiply, and increase in you, to your great content and satisfaction. But the thoughts of the wicked are sin, and sin brings trouble, anguish and torment; men are accused or excused in their thoughts. It is said *Belshazzer* was so much troubled with his thoughts, *that his countenance was changed, and the joints of his loins were loosed, and his knees smote together.* Many are the amazing tormenting thoughts that attend the wicked, *whose feet run to do evil, and make haste to shed innocent blood; their thoughts are thoughts of iniquity; wasting and destruction are in their paths; the way of peace they know not; and there is no judgment in their goings.*

Now the thoughts of the righteous are right, and those that commit their way to the Lord, their thoughts shall be established: and that is a blessed state indeed; to have good thoughts established in the heart, in the mind, such can go forth, and come in, in peace, lie down and rise up in peace, live and walk in peace, and praise the God of peace, who is blessed for evermore: and this is the peace, the inward peace, which the world with all its treasures and pleasures cannot give, nor by its frowns take away, and is the portion of all that get victory over their own thoughts, imaginations, lusts, desires and affections; and that do also keep in the wisdom and Power of God, that when good thoughts are established in them, and are so made partakers of the divine nature, that they naturally think good thoughts, thoughts of Love, peace, and obedience, as they did while in the degeneration think the contrary; yet in this state of innocence and harmlessness be diligent in the wisdom of God, to dress and keep the Garden, lest you having found honey, eat more than may suffice to nourish the right birth, lest you feed yourself without fear, eat and drink and rise up to play, grow idle and wanton, through plenty, and so forget the Lord, and let his

---

[7] *Prov. xv. 29. Dan. v. 6. Isa. lix. 7, 8.*

[8] *Good thoughts are of God's own begetting and very comfortable to a Christian, and are the fruit and effect of keeping and obeying the law of God within the heart, Rom, ii. 14. 15.*

benefits slip out of your mind, and slight his commandments, and let pride and exaltation in your selfish spirit grow up again, as the first *Adam* and others did, mentioned in the holy scriptures, which are written for *our learning and admonition; upon whom the ends of the world are come*; therefore *let him that thinks he stands, take heed lest he fall*[9].

---

[9] *1 Cor. x. ii.*

CONCERNING THE LIFE, STATE AND ENJOYMENT OF A TRUE CHRISTIAN.

The life of a Christian, of an Israelite indeed, in whom is no guile, is a life of innocence, peace and contentment; quietness and true satisfaction abounds in the inward man, so none can harm him; he lives in the fear of God, which taught him to depart from iniquity, and now preserves him out of the same, he loves God and his neighbor, and hates no man, so fears not what man can do unto him; his bread is sure, and his water fails not: if he has wife or children, house or land, or the increase of corn, wine and oil, he looks upon them as things below, so does not set his heart and affection upon them; he looks upon them as they are, and loves them in their places, but not more than Christ: he loves the Lord above all, he loves to keep his conscience void of offence towards God, and towards man, above all; and if he cannot enjoy his estate and relations according to the will of God, he is ready and willing to part with them, and can say as *Job* did, *The Lord giveth, and the Lord taketh away; blessed be the name of the Lord.* He is not afraid of evil tidings; the ruffling of the winds, and the roaring of the sea, does not amaze nor frighten him; he lives the life of faith, which gives him victory, and enables him to overcome all things, he keeps on the helmet of it, and the breast-plate of righteousness, and the sword of the Spirit, so is always armed against all assaults of the world, flesh, and the devil; and he knows the name of the Lord as a strong tower, as a shield, as a buckler, as a wall of defense, and is prepared to suffer and endure all things, like good soldiers, with a settled countenance, and holy resolution: and though by men he may be accounted smitten and forsaken of God, and not fit to live upon the earth, yet he enjoys heavenly consolation, pure tranquility of mind, refreshment, comfort, and joy in the inward man; the king's daughter is all glorious within, and all things that do, or can befall a *Christian* on this side the grave, are not worthy to be compared to the glory *that is and shall be revealed in him*: and if there was no reward on the other side the grave, he would not exchange his life and condition, for all the glory, riches, and excellency the world can afford, seeing and accounting it all vanity and vexation of spirit, yes, less than nothing, and lighter than vanity. (Psalm lxii. 9) Having found the precious pearl, which the swine regard not, he is willing to part with all for it, knowing the wonderful virtue, riches, and power thereof, bids adieu to all the fading treasures and pleasures of *Egypt*; (Isa. xi.16) choosing rather to suffer affliction and persecution for righteousness sake, than to enjoy the court pleasures of princes; and he is a great gainer hereby, specifically in this life, on this side of the grave, a hundred-fold: he finds by experience that saying true, *godliness with contentment is great gain; and is profitable unto all things, having the promise of the life that now is, and of that which is to come.* (1 Tim. iv. 6)

So though the true *Christian* seems, in the judgment of the wise in their conceit, to lose the enjoyment of his life, honor, riches, profit, pleasure, preferment, relations, et cetera, instead thereof he finds them all; and in the true self-denial enjoys them all, and is able to say as Paul did to the *Corinthians*, speaking of himself and other *Christians, as sorrowful, yet always rejoicing; as poor, yet making many rich; as having nothing, yet possessing all things; having learned to be content in all estates and conditions, Knowing how to suffer want, and how to abound, everywhere, and in all things.* And where there is true contentment, there is no want, no poverty no sorrow, but what is turned into plenty, riches, and rejoicing. It makes him rejoice in sorrow, sing in the stocks, makes a dungeon a palace, bonds and chains liberty; makes poverty riches, turns loss into gain, darkness into light before him; these and many more are the virtues and powerful operations of the precious pearl, the white stone, the elect and precious stone, the chief corner stone, which the wise master builders set at naught and stumble at, and will not use in their building; but to the *Christian* indeed he is precious, he is his foundation, corner and top stone also; and as a treasure better than mountains of Gold, and as a rock out of which issues the water of life, that makes the river of pleasure, that never ceases running at the right-hand of God: these things are known and enjoyed by the true *Christian*, as he arrives at the mark of the high calling of God in Christ Jesus, and they who are but travelers therein, taste of the same in the way thereto; but the bare professor, or titular *Christian*, knows nothing hereof; for, the life, riches, and enjoyment of a *Christian* is inward and hidden; his life is hid with Christ in God, none know it but he that has it; his conversation is with God in Heaven, and his treasure is laid up where he walks and dwells, and where he sits in heavenly places with his Savior Christ Jesus, who is made unto him wisdom, righteousness, sanctification and redemption; and not only so, but he is come to

A True Christian

see what is the fellowship of the mystery which from *the beginning of the world has been hid in God*; he is come to know *the Lord one, and his name one; to the one body, one Spirit, one hope, one faith, one baptism, one way, one truth, one life, one God and Father of all, who is above all, through all, and in all.* This is the blessed end of all the appearances, manifestations and dispensations, under all the variety of names, and various workings of the one eternal God towards mankind ever since the fall, mentioned throughout the holy scriptures, and witnessed to by the true *Christian*, who really enjoys the end of *Paul's* bowing his knees, or prayer unto the Father of our Lord Jesus Christ, of whom the whole family in Heaven and Earth is named. (Ephes, iii, 14, 15)

Now when the true *Christian* has known a being dead and buried with, and a rising with him; and not only seeking those things that are above, but has found them, having known and experienced Christ in all his offices, as the great ordinance of God, as a mediator, reconciler, intercessor, makes of peace, healer of the wound, and maker up of the breach the first *Adam* made, as a quickening spirit, and Lord from Heaven; as a king, priest and prophet; as a Savior, sanctifier and Redeemer; as a purifier and maker an end of sin, and bringer in of everlasting righteousness; and as a high priest to present to God without spot or wrinkle, or any such thing: when he is thus known to perform all these offices in and for his people, he is then by such known to sit down at the right hand of God, having accomplished the work the Father gave him to do, having put all things under, and restored all things into their primitive order; he then is also known to surrender up the kingdom to the father, and God to become all in all: here the first is known to be last, and the last first; the beginning the end, and end the beginning; and the heavenly rest with him who is without beginning or end: I say, rest with him, in a pure celestial stillness, from all self working, willing, running, and thinking; and though an innocence, or innocent self be attained unto, and a harmless will known, yet that must not act, work, will, run and think of itself, as the true *Christian*, who has traveled and experienced, as before is hinted, knows right well; saying to his Father, *not my will but thine*: herein he receives wisdom to dress and keep the garden, power and strength to resist and overcome the serpent in paradise, and the dragon in heaven, and to keep his habitation in the heavenly city *Jerusalem*, which comes down from God out of Heaven, whose walls are salvation, and whose gates are praise for ever.

CONCERNING
CHRISTIAN WORSHIP,
WHAT IT STANDS IN,
And how it is performed.

There is a great contest in *Christendom* among the diverse sects and bare profession of *Christianity* about worship; and many are the modes and ceremonies that are cried up among them; every sect conceiving their way to be right, all being full of dispute, contention, and quarrelling one with and against another, envying and hating one another, fighting, killing and destroying one another about them when they are all but of their own devising, forms and images of their own making, mostly from the example of *Jews*, *Gentiles*, and apostate *Christians*, and are not led thereto, nor guided therein by the unerring Spirit of God, as their fruits make fully manifest, to the great scandal of the *Christian* religion.

Now the true *Christian* worship is in the Spirit, and in the truth, not in the letter, nor in the form barely, but was before all letters and outward laws and prescriptions, inventions, errors, and the spirit of them, was: this was the worship in paradise; when mankind neglected this worship he fell into evil, into invention, into error, which was the cause of the outward law, and all other dispensations of God, for the recovery of lost man: and before he can witness a return out of his lost estate, he must come again to the same, worship in the Spirit and in the truth, specifically the truth in the inward parts, for that is it which God loves; to the word in the mouth, to the law in the heart, and the fear in the inward parts, from all fear towards God, taught by the precepts of men, from all traditions of men of corrupt minds from all devices and inventions of men: this is the blessed estate the true *Christian* is come into, and is the end, sum, and substance of all holy writings, forms, and holy traditions, ministrations, and dispensations before the law, under the law and the prophets: wilderness *Jerusalem*, and temple-worship, which stood in diverse bodily exercises, outward works and services, variety of offerings, observing of times, days, months, and years, meats, drinks, outward washings and purifications, new moons, fasts, feasts, solemn meetings and general assemblies once a year at

Christian Worship

Jerusalem; all these things were but shadows and typical; and this is the antitype and substance shadowed forth by them all. To come to the worship in the *Spirit, in the Truth* to *Mount Zion*, the city of the living God, the heavenly *Jerusalem*; and *to come to the general assembly and church of the first born, written in Heaven, and to God the judge of all and the spirits of just men made perfect.* To know the heavenly city that comes down from God out of Heaven, specifically *Jerusalem* the mother of all the living citizens thereof, whose law and covenant is spiritual; and writ in their hearts; whose love, fear, and obedience to God, is engraved in their inward parts; and from hence arises the true worship in the Spirit and in the truth.

This is the worship the primitive *Christians* came to, and were exercised in; they prayed in the Spirit, not at any set time, or appointed place only, according to the exhortations, *pray always, pray continually, pray without ceasing; I will that men pray every where, lifting up holy hands without wrath or doubting*; breathing to the Lord in Spirit, though never a word be uttered; in the closet when the door is shut, the Lord hears, and answers this prayer. And many times they were, and are also led forth to pray in words publicly, but mostly for the sake of others and in the behalf of others, as Christ Jesus did.

The true *Christian*, is also a preacher of righteousness, not only in words, at set times, and appointed places, but in life and conversation; in this he is a preacher, a teacher of that which is good, as a candle burning and set in the right place; his lamp trimmed, and his light shining; as a city upon a hill, as the salt of the earth, and light of the world, to season and give light to others, by holy example, which preaches louder than words.

The true *Christians* singing or rejoicing is also in the Spirit and in the truth, and not in iniquity, and with a good understanding; he needs no are nor invention to bring words into meter or rhyme, that they may make a pleasant sound, and a joyful noise; his music does not stand in outward sounds, made by art and air, but his melody is in the heart, in the spirit, in the inward man, in the hidden man of the heart, which is the antitype and substance of all outward music used in the time of the law, under the first covenant, in the worship and service of God; and as far exceeds it, as the substance of a thing does the shadow thereof: and he that has this heavenly inward rejoicing, and pleasant melody in the heart, will never invent to himself instruments of music like *David*, nor delight in the sounds thereof. Where this heart melody is lost, the

Christian Worship

outward invented music is set up, among *Jews, Gentiles,* and apostate *Christians;* for the *Christian* is come to know Christ Jesus as a Prince of Peace, as a peaceable Savior, as the consolation of *Israel,* and joy of generations; as a giver of peace, which the world cannot give or take away, which far surpasses all the delights of the sons of men, which by nature, are and invention, they can attain unto.

Now the Spirit of God is universal, and the truth is universal, and the true *Christian* worship that stands in it, is also to be universal, not only when people meet together in a solemn manner to wait upon God, but every hour and every day, bowing in spirit, worshipping in the truth, which make free from all error, from all evil, from all vain observations, literal traditions, and human inventions about the worship of God, from all carnal ordinances, as *music, meats, drinking, washings, feasts, fasts, days and times,* which perish with the using, though significant in their first institution; these things are not to be touched, nor tasted, no nor so much as handled by the true *Christian;* these things are but beggarly elements, and worldly rudiments, which had a beginning, and must have an end.

And the root or cause of a *Christian,* which is Christ, is the end of the law, and all the types and shadows of it, and fulfils all the righteousness of it, of the prophets, and of *John* also, and is a bringer in of a better hope, a better law, a better covenant, a better worship; which hope, law, covenant and worship, is inward and spiritual, and not outward and carnal, formal nor traditional: and all that are come to this worship in the Spirit, and in the truth, which is one pure eternal principle of light, life and power, and have their hearts tendered by it, and their minds exercised in it, their thoughts and meditations guided by it, they are come to the mystery of the fellowship of the gospel, to the blessed unity wherein is no strife, no wrangling, disputing, or contention; no treachery, wars, cruelty, or violence; because they are all minding one thing, learning of one teacher, following of one guide, *namely,* the Grace and Spirit of God: and though they have diversity of gifts, and are attained to different degrees of faith, of grace, of knowledge, growth and salvation in the same; and are some as a foot, some as a hand, eye, ear and mouth, yet are all as members of one body; and the meanest has unity with the more noble, the greatest with the least, the lowest with the highest, and strongest with the weakest. Nor is there any jar or schism, in this well-framed body, of which, Christ, the unction, the anointing, is the head and teacher.

Christian Worship

This heavenly unity is the antitype of the seamless coat of Christ, wove from top to bottom, which the soldiers did not rend, tear, or divide, but cast lots for, and of that law that forbade *weaving linen* and *woolen* together, and *sowing mingled seed*.

Now there is no concord between light and darkness, sin and righteousness, Christ and Belial; these things of a *different* and *contrary nature*, cannot unite, cannot agree, though they are near to each other, sown in one field. God has sown a good seed in the field of mankind; the enemy has sown an evil seed, and in many it has taken root, and sprung up above the good seed, specifically among those professing *Christianity* itself; and from hence arises and grows all the evil will, envy, hatred, strife, cruelty, violence, bloodshed, wars and murders in the world, and till the head of this evil seed be not only bruised, by the promised seed which God has sowed, but rooted out also of the heart of man, all these things will grow up; these evil effects can never cease till the cause be removed, and taken away, as the true *Christian* knows right well by experience.

Now the *Christians* indeed, as they live and abide in this pure *internal principle* of light, life, Spirit, and truth, they have unity one with another, and fellowship with God: they are the brethren whose living together in unity is comely to behold, who have the one mind, one heart; and have their minds and hearts always governed, ruled and ordered by the good Spirit of God: as every one lives and keeps this order, and under this heavenly government they cannot but live together in unity, in love, in good-will, in peace, heavenly concord and agreement, every one within himself, with God, and with each other, and in love to all mankind; here is the end of strife, wars and fighting come unto, both within and without; and this is the time and state wherein *instruments of war and cruelty* are turned into *instruments of necessary use*; and as they abide herein, they can learn war no more, according to the blessed sight and prophesy of *Isaiah*, that Evangelical prophet. Here *Jerusalem* is known a *quiet habitation*, the inhabitants thereof being established in *peace and righteousness*, far from oppressing, the cause of war and oppression being taken away, which is *evil-thinking, evil-speaking*, and *evil doing*; and this every one must know and experience before they can be established in peace; before they can know the peace of God which passes all understanding, to keep their hearts and minds, and to rule in their hearts, and to know the abounding of it, and to delight therein; as it is written, *the meek shall inherit the earth, and delight themselves*

Christian Worship

in the abundance of peace; the earth, or earthly things, shall not inherit them; they tread upon the high places of it, and reign like kings and princes over all the glory thereof. Oh! this is a blessed state indeed; wait all to possess and enjoy it more and more, this is the blessed end of the gospel of peace, and of the Christian Religion. My breathing is, that all that profess it, may come to inherit peace, righteousness, and joy in the inward man; specifically to lie down in that peace where none can make afraid, and to dwell on that holy mountain where no destroyer is, and to inhabit that city whose builder and maker is God: to whom be praise and glory for evermore.

A FEW WORDS ADDED
TO THE
SENSIBLE READER

You who are awakened out of the sleep of death, and risen out of the grave of sin, and sea of corruption, and are come to the exercise of your spiritual senses, so that you can hear, see, taste, and handle the things of God, you well knows that the blessed end of all holy men's words and writings, testimonies and declarations, proceeding from the love of God, is, that others that are yet unholy, wandering about in and after the vanity of their own minds, thoughts, and imaginations, upon the barren mountains, even as sheep without a shepherd, may come to be gathered and brought home to the fold of rest, where safety, peace, and satisfaction is to be found for their weary souls, who have long wandered in desolate places, seeking rest, but finding none; spending their time, labor, and money for that which does not profit, feed, and nourish up to eternal life. I say, to direct these strangers, wanderers, laborers, and unsatisfied travelers into the way of rest and peace, is the blessed end of all words and holy writings, specifically that such may come to possess, enjoy, and inherit the things spoken, and written of; without which, all hearing, reading, seeking, enquiring, toiling, laboring, spending time and money is to no purpose.

Now it is the soul of man that lacks rest, that is gone from his centre, that has lost its stay, habitation, and dwelling-place in God; and innumerable are the thoughts, imaginations, devices and inventions wiling and running that poor mankind in this estate is exercised in, and carried away with, both *Jew* and *Gentile*, professor and profane, upon the face of the whole earth: for in all sects and sorts of religions, those who are sincere and devout therein, purpose this end to themselves in the exercise thereof, *that is to say*, to attain a state of happiness and felicity at last: many are the ways, means, and precepts, prescriptions, directions, and observations, that men give and receive from one another, enjoin and persuade one another, and sometimes compel one another by violence to walk in, and make use of, in order to arrive thereto, as they think and imagine; but it is in this age, as of old, the guides and teachers of the people cause them to err, cause them to go astray, and wander from the right way of the Lord; they err in vision, judgment, and understanding themselves, and cause all that follow and obey them to do the same being unskillful guides, and blind watchmen, are but as the blind leading the blind, and so both fall into the ditch together.

Now the way to everlasting happiness is but one, both the *Jew* and *Gentile*; which way is Christ, who is the wisdom and Power of God, the truth, and the life; and the appearance of this Christ, of God, is within men, in their hearts: his first appearance is as a light shining in darkness, and as a pure spotless spirit that consents to no evil, but reproves and convinces all that are found in it; and to this light or spirit, all who write or speak for God, and the good of mankind, do turn and direct the minds of men, and endeavor to persuade them to regard its reproofs of instruction, as being the way to life, and to obey its counsel and teaching, as the only means of salvation, and way of returning to the rock from whence they were hewn, and to the hole of the pit from whence they were dug, to their habitation, and dwelling-place in God again, and many thousands in this island and other places, can give testimony that this is the only way and means God has ordained for the recovery, return, and restoration of lost man; and that all other ways and means which they had been wearying themselves in, availed nothing; but walking in this heavenly way, the light, the Spirit and grace of God within, and learning of the anointing within, they witness salvation come to their house, and to surround them as walls and bulwarks, and to witness the fulfilling of that divine prophecy, *my people shall dwell in a peaceable habitation, and in sure dwellings, and in quiet resting places. The eye of them that see shall not be dim, the ear of them that hear shall hearken, the heart also of the rash shall understand knowledge, and the tongue of them that stammer, shall be ready to speak plainly.* These are the blessed effects of walking in the way and paths of righteousness, which a remnant are living witnesses of, and can praise and magnify the name of the Lord in the sense thereof.

But none enjoy this blessed estate, nor inhabit this heavenly dwelling-place, but as their minds come truly to be exercised by and in the light of the Lord; and that by walking and abiding therein, come to have their minds established, settled, and stayed upon him, who is indeed the alone stay of his people, and rock of his inheritance.

And nothing can be found in the heavens above, nor in the earth beneath, that is able to satisfy or stay the mind of man, but the Lord; the mind or soul of man is more noble, more excellent than all visible things, so they are not all

To The Sensible Reader

capable to fill or satisfy his soul, or stay his mind, though he might possess or have the whole world to himself, yet in the end will be made to cry out and confess with the preacher of old, *vanity of vanities, all is vanity and vexation of spirit*. But in having the mind stayed upon the Lord, there is pleasure, peace and content, truly found and enjoyed, according to the testimony of that divine prophet *Isaiah*, who said, speaking in the name of the Lord, *you will keep him in perfect peace, whose mind is stayed upon you*. This is a truth, that none know but he that has it; it may be soon writ, read, or spoken, but to enjoy that estate is more than words, it is the end, sum and substance of all that can be said or done, and is the reward of the righteous from the immediate hand of God, *namely, to be kept, in perfect peace*: it is the end of all holy breathings and desires, it is the end of the preaching the gospel of peace and salvation, specifically to know and feel, and experience the peace of God to keep the heart and mind, and to rule there.

This is a blessed state indeed, worthy to be waited for, and pressed after, by all that have a sight and sense thereof, and are in a way that leads thereto, though not yet arrived thereat: go forward in the name of the Lord, specifically in that name, *light*, by which he has made himself known unto us in this age, by which light you saw the wandering and unstableness of your mind, and the multitude of your thoughts, imaginations and inventions; persevere in the same, and you will become not only a child of it, but also grow from a child's estate to the state of a young man, elder, and father: *keeping the faith*, and *firmly believing*, that which showed you the *wandering* and *unstableness* of your mind, will be as a shepherd's crook unto you, and in due time will bring you back into the fold of rest; and that holy light that discovers, and shows unto you your thoughts, and inward enemies, will also by the brightness of its arising, disperse and destroy them for you, and bring you into that estate your soul desires, pants and looks after, specifically into the *presence* of the *Lord*, where the fullness of joy is, and where the rivers of pleasure run; where the reaping and returning with joy is, where the singing for joy of heart is, and the joy of God's salvation is felt; the blessed light of God, or sun of righteousness, in whom you hast believed, is the only way to *possess* and *inherit* these things. And your *walking abiding*, and *persevering* in it, is the means, and there is not any other *way* or *means* appointed of God, to bring man back into that paradisiacal state of felicity he lost by transgression, and to the *establishing* him in it.

To The Sensible Reader

But all that walk not, nor abide and persevere therein, after they are come into it, never attain to that blessed end of its appearing and shining to them; for a bare knowledge of the truth, and a profession of the light and Spirit of God within, if they walk not in it, and are not guided and lead by it, avails nothing, but rather draws down fierce wrath and vengeance upon the head of such, who know their master's will and do it not, who talk and profess well, but are found *doing evil*, and thereby lay a *stumbling-block* in the way of the blind, and cause the way of truth to be *evil spoken* of, and the name of the Lord, by which he has made himself known in this age, to be *blasphemed*, by reason of their *ungodly deeds*, under a profession of godliness, and cloak of righteousness; the *damnation* of such slumbers not.

And this I testify and declare, to all people to whom this may come, which may serve also as a *caution* and *warning* to them, that if they meet with any under the name, form, and profession of a Christian, in contempt called a Quaker, who in his converse, trade and dealing, commerce and affairs, does not let his yes be yes, and his nay, nay, but breaks his word and promises, there is need to have a special care of that man, and look upon him as one false and deceitful to the holy principle of truth, and as a hypocrite, under the profession of it. He that is false to God, cannot be true to men; you had better trust and give credit to a Heathen or Infidel, than to such a one. No wickedness beyond that which is acted under a peculiar cloak of religion. Such who gain credit and repute by wearing this cloak, and get widows and orphans' monies, into their hands, to create great trades by sea and land, are some of the worse sort of robbers and cheats, and the cry of the poor fatherless and widows cries loud against them. This is a short testimony arising in my heart against this sort of wickedness, wherein I have a little eased my mind, and in the truth, remain a friend to all men.

W. SHEWEN.

Printed in the United States
141731LV00008B/60/P